THE USBORNE BOOK OF
PAPERCRAFT

Edited by Alastair Smith
Designed by Fiona Brown and Nigel Reece

Material in this book originally developed by
Paula Borton, Annabelle Curtis, Cheryl Evans,
Felicity Everett, Carol Garbera, Ray Gibson, Judy Hindley,
Peter Holland, Susan Mayes, Kate Needham, Clare Rosen,
Anna Rowley, Louisa Somerville, Jenny Tyler and Fiona Watt

Illustrated by
Simone Abel, Chris Chaisty, Prue Greener,
Colin King, Angie Sage, Guy Smith, Sue Stitt,
Lily Whitlock and Jonathon Woodcock

Photography by
Howard Allman, Amanda Heywood and Ray Moller

Models made by
Fiona Brown, Lindy Dark, Non Figg, Kathy Gemmell, Emma Jones,
Patricia Lovett, Anna Rowley and Helen Westwood

This edition first published in 1995 by Usborne Publishing Ltd, Usborne House, 83-85 Saffron Hill, London, EC1N 8RT, England.
Copyright © Usborne Publishing Ltd, 2001, 1995, 1994, 1993, 1992, 1990, 1989, 1987, 1984, 1975.

Printed in Italy.
UE First printed in America, March 1996.

THE USBORNE
BIG
BOOK OF
PAPERCRAFT

Contents

PAPER FUN

This section contains all sorts of projects that are fun to make and just as much fun to use. Almost everything you need to know is explained as you follow the instructions – although there is some general information that you might find useful on pages 86-87.

For some projects you will need templates that appear on pages 88-91.

⚠

To avoid harming yourself take extra care when you see a red warning triangle.

Painted paper plates

You can create some amazing effects on paper objects, such as paper plates, by attaching masking tape to them and painting them with layers of bright paint. If you like the effect, you could use it on other projects that you'll find in this book.

Decorating the plates

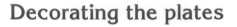

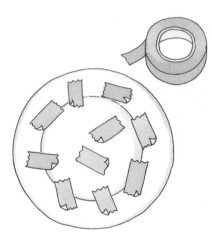

Always start with light shades and go on to the darker shades later.

1. Tear off ten pieces of masking tape, each about 3cm (1in) long. Put them on a paper plate, leaving a corner of each piece sticking up.

2. In the yogurt cartons, mix each paint with some water. Make sure you add plenty of water to make the mixed paint fairly runny.

3. Start by brushing paint over the whole plate and all the pieces of tape. Then leave the plate in a warm place to allow the paint to dry.

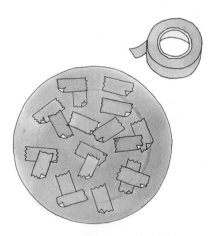

Don't forget to clean your brush between each coat of paint.

4. When it has dried, press about ten more pieces of tape onto the plate. The fresh pieces can overlap painted ones, but don't cover them completely.

5. Now cover the whole plate with a different shade of paint and leave it somewhere warm until it is dry, ready for the next stage.

6. Repeat the process over and over. When your final layer of paint is dry, peel the pieces of tape away to reveal the decorations beneath.

You could coat your plate
in varnish to give it a
polished look.

You might
like to hang
the plate on
a wall in your
room to make an
interesting decoration.

You don't
have to take
off all the
tape, if you
find a pattern
you like.

Other ideas

Use pale pink paint for the first layer, then mix a little red into the following coats. The final layer of paint should be pure red. You could experiment with different shades of blue, green or orange.

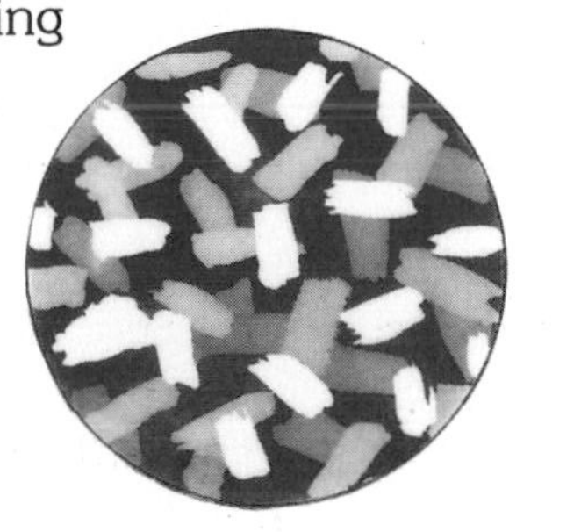

Cut the masking tape into shapes, such as diamonds or triangles, to make patterns on your plate. To make the cutting easier draw on lines beforehand.

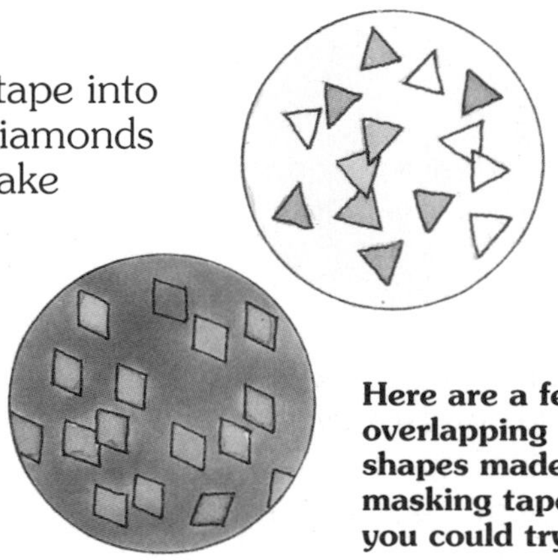

Here are a few overlapping shapes made with masking tape that you could try.

Viking ship

Origami is a Japanese word that means "paper folding". The ancient Japanese invented the technique to make paper decorations for special ceremonies. You can use the same basic folds to make the Viking ship model shown here.

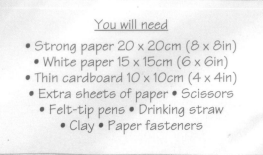
Making the ship's hull

These symbols are explained on page 87.

1. Fold the square of strong paper in half from side to side, as shown above.

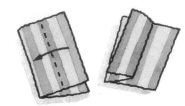

2. Fold the right hand edge back to meet the fold that you made in the first stage.

3. Turn the paper over. Fold the right edge back to the folded edge. Then unfold it.

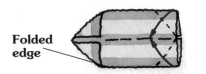

Folded edge

4. Fold the four corners into the middle crease so that both ends are pointed.

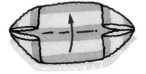

5. Fold the top edge back to the folded edge of the paper, to make the shape shown above.

6. Press all the folds down firmly to give the shape some sharp, neat creases.

7. Hold the paper as shown above. Put your fingers inside and your thumb 0.5cm (¼in) from the top of the side fold.

8. With your other hand, push the corner over your thumbnail. Then squash the corner down flat to the ship's bottom.

9. Fold the other corner in the same way, so that the paper becomes a ship shape.

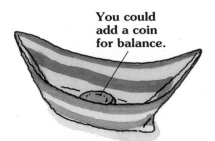

You could add a coin for balance.

10. Turn the ship over and float it. It will sail best with something inside.

Making the sail

1. Press some clay down into the bottom of the ship. Stand a drinking straw in it for the mast.

Add stripes on the sail using felt-tips.

2. Make a sail from a square of paper 15 x 15cm (6 x 6in). Thread it onto the mast.

Making the figurehead

Trace the outline of this dragon onto some thin cardboard (don't make it too heavy or it might capsize your boat). Then decorate it on both sides. When you have finished decorating the dragon make a slit in the neck and slot it onto the front of the ship.

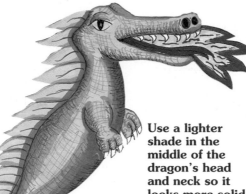

Use a lighter shade in the middle of the dragon's head and neck so it looks more solid.

The Vikings put figureheads on many of their ships. They usually carved them from wood and nailed them to the front of the hull. They believed that the figureheads brought them good luck during their long voyages.

You might like to put shields on the side of your ship. Copy the ones shown here and fasten them onto the ship using paper fasteners.

If you want to display your ship you could put some stylized wave shapes around it, as shown here.

Paper pencil tops

You can brighten up pencils by adding funny-looking animals to their tops. Besides the ones shown here you could make pencil tops that look like other creatures such as a horse, a cow or an elephant. There are templates for the frog, cat, rabbit, duck and pig on page 89 for you to trace.

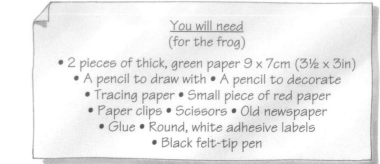

You will need
(for the frog)
• 2 pieces of thick, green paper 9 x 7cm (3½ x 3in)
• A pencil to draw with • A pencil to decorate
• Tracing paper • Small piece of red paper
• Paper clips • Scissors • Old newspaper
• Glue • Round, white adhesive labels
• Black felt-tip pen

Frog

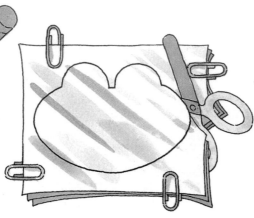

1. Lay tracing paper over the frog template. Trace around the outline and the features using a soft pencil.

2. Fasten the tracing onto two layers of green paper using paper clips. Cut out the head and remove the tracing paper.

3. Working on old newspaper, spread a layer of glue on each cut-out shape. Spread evenly to cover to the edges.

At the back, press the paper around the pencil.

4. Spread glue over 3cm (1in) of the unsharpened end of a new pencil. Lay the glued end onto one shape, as shown.

5. Carefully press the second shape on top and ease the edges so that they meet exactly. Allow the glue to dry.

6. Press on two labels for eyes, as shown. Mark in the middles with a black felt-tip pen, to give the eyes pupils.

7. Add a wide mouth and nostrils. Glue on a bow tie cut from a piece of red paper.

You could draw eyes like these to give your frog a sleepy look.

8. Finally, glue two or three tiny pieces of red paper onto the pencil, just below the bow tie. These will look like buttons.

Other ideas to try

Badges

Tape a safety pin onto a face made from a single layer of cardboard.

Hairband

Glue a face made from a single layer of paper onto a hairband.

Finger puppet

Leave an unglued area at the bottom of the head big enough to insert a finger.

More pencil tops

Rabbit

Make a rabbit face out of white paper. Use pink paper for the nose and inner ears. Draw in the face with a black felt-tip pen.

Pig

Use pink paper for a pig. Glue on ears and a snout. Use half labels for eyes. Mark in the eyes and nose with a felt-tip pen.

Cat

You could use white paper to make a cat face, and then decorate it so that it looks like a cat that you've seen.

Duck

Cut out a yellow face using the duck template. Glue on an orange beak and use labels to make the eyes. Mark the face as shown here.

Origami water bomb

By following these instructions you can make water-tight cubes that you could use as water bombs. They will explode and soak whatever target they hit, so it's best to use them outdoors, to avoid causing too much mess.

You will need

• Paper, at least 12 x 12 cm (5 x 5in) (decorated wrapping paper is ideal because it is eye-catching and fairly strong)

Making the bomb

These symbols are explained on page 87.

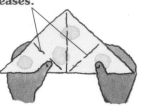

Hold below these creases.

1. Fold the paper in half from side to side and then from bottom to top. Unfold it and turn it over.

2. Turn one corner so that it points to you. Fold the side corners together and then unfold them.

3. Fold the bottom corner to the top corner. Pick up the paper and hold it at the bottom edge.

4. Holding the bottom edge, push in gently. The top corners should move out and the side ones should move in.

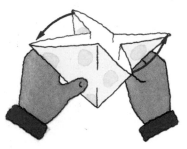

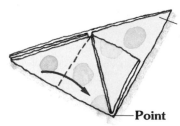

Leave this corner on the table.

Point

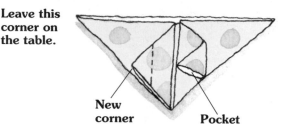

New corner

Pocket

5. Fold the front corner to one side and the back corner to the other side.

6. Press the paper flat on a table. Then fold the top two corners to the bottom point.

7. Fold the new corners into the middle. Look for the little pockets that you make when you do this. You will need to use them in the next stage of this project.

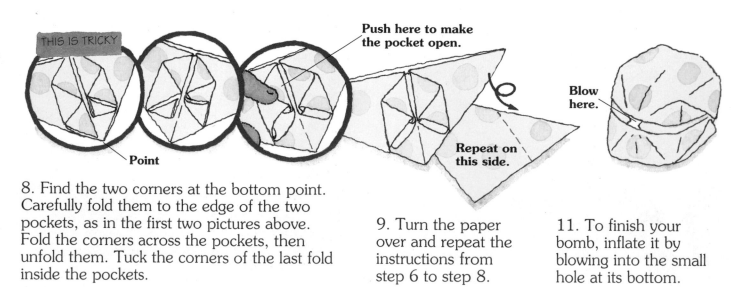

THIS IS TRICKY

Push here to make the pocket open.

Point

Repeat on this side.

Blow here.

8. Find the two corners at the bottom point. Carefully fold them to the edge of the two pockets, as in the first two pictures above. Fold the corners across the pockets, then unfold them. Tuck the corners of the last fold inside the pockets.

9. Turn the paper over and repeat the instructions from step 6 to step 8.

11. To finish your bomb, inflate it by blowing into the small hole at its bottom.

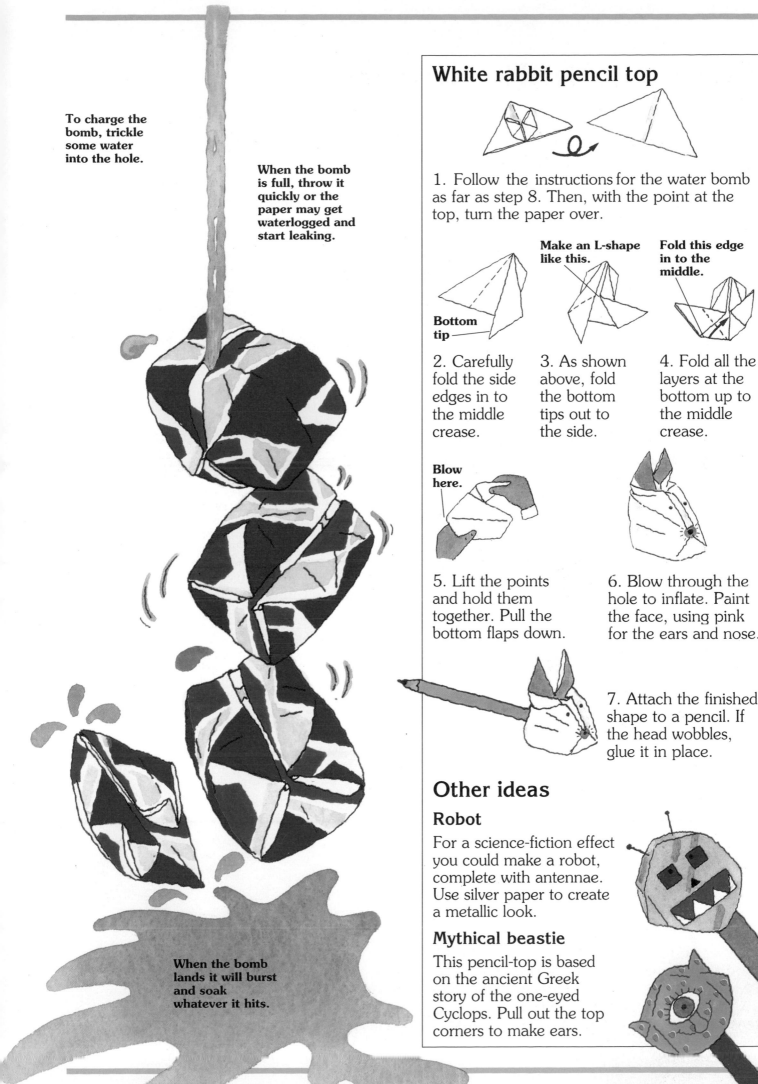

To charge the bomb, trickle some water into the hole.

When the bomb is full, throw it quickly or the paper may get waterlogged and start leaking.

When the bomb lands it will burst and soak whatever it hits.

White rabbit pencil top

1. Follow the instructions for the water bomb as far as step 8. Then, with the point at the top, turn the paper over.

Make an L-shape like this.

Fold this edge in to the middle.

Bottom tip

2. Carefully fold the side edges in to the middle crease.

3. As shown above, fold the bottom tips out to the side.

4. Fold all the layers at the bottom up to the middle crease.

Blow here.

5. Lift the points and hold them together. Pull the bottom flaps down.

6. Blow through the hole to inflate. Paint the face, using pink for the ears and nose.

7. Attach the finished shape to a pencil. If the head wobbles, glue it in place.

Other ideas

Robot

For a science-fiction effect you could make a robot, complete with antennae. Use silver paper to create a metallic look.

Mythical beastie

This pencil-top is based on the ancient Greek story of the one-eyed Cyclops. Pull out the top corners to make ears.

Waste papercraft

You can use pieces of waste paper, such as old newspapers or postcards, to create instant works of art or to perform amazing tricks.

Magic ladder

1. First lay out two sheets of old newspaper, with their ends overlapping. Then roll them up and fasten their ends with adhesive tape.

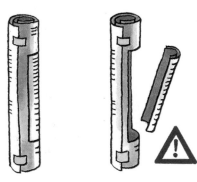

2. Mark a section on the tube of newspaper, as shown above left. The section should go almost half way around the tube. Then cut out the section.

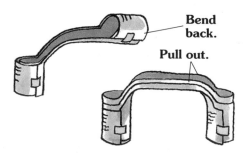

Bend back.

Pull out.

3. Bend the tube back to make a bridge shape. Gently pull out the insides from each side. The ladder will emerge from this shape.

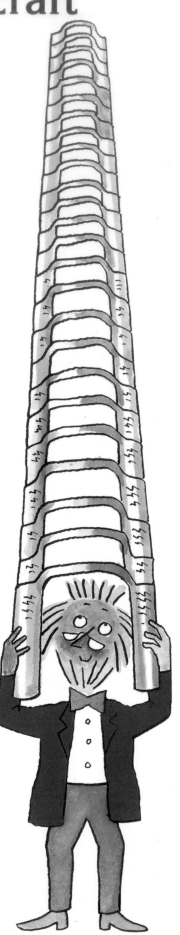

You could use more than two sheets to make a really high ladder.

You will need
• A newspaper • Pen
• 2 strips of paper 40cm (16in) long
• Adhesive tape
• Stiff yellow paper
• Postcard • Scissors

Amazing loops

Single-twist loop

1. Take a strip of paper around 40cm (16in) long. Twist it by turning one end over, then tape it into a loop. Mark a dot on the outside of the loop.

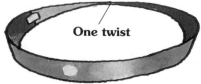

One twist

2. Hold the dot between your finger and thumb, with your thumb on the dot. Run the tape between your finger and thumb, until the dot is back between them. A surprising thing will have happened.

Double-twist loop

1. Take another long strip of paper and put two twists in it by turning one end over twice. Tape it into a loop.

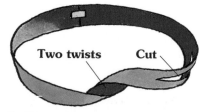

Two twists   **Cut**

2. Using scissors, make a cut in the middle of the loop, as shown above. Keep on cutting until you've cut all around it. The result will probably surprise you.

Wild paper tree

1. Lay out two sheets of newspaper, with their ends overlapping. Roll them up and fasten adhesive tape across the middle and one end of the tube.

2. Starting at the end that isn't taped, make cuts down either side of the newspaper tube. Each of the cuts should be about 15cm (6in) long.

 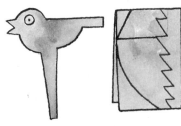

3. Make two more 15cm (6in) long cuts halfway between the first two cuts. Make sure that the paper flops down, as shown in the picture.

4. Reach inside and, little by little, gently pull the insides of the tube up and out. Your wild paper tree will grow right in front of your eyes.

To make your finished tree look more decorative, you could spray or paint it.

Making the bird

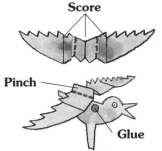

Score

Pinch

Glue

1. Copy the long-legged bird template onto some stiff paper and cut it out. Trace the wing template onto some stiff folded paper. (Both templates are on page 89.)

2. Unfold the wings and score as shown. Fold each side toward the middle. Put glue on each side of the back, pinch on the wing and poke the leg into the top of the tree.

Walk-through postcard

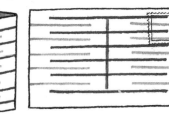

1. Fold a postcard in half. Make cuts, shown in red, from the fold almost to the edges. Make cuts, shown in green, from the edges almost to the fold.

2. Open the card out and cut along the fold, as indicated by the blue line. Then tug the card so it falls open. Can you fit your body through the hole?

Paper houses

Once you have made a house to the size given in the instructions, you could go on to build others in different shapes and sizes. You might like to create a model village and decorate the houses to look like buildings you have seen.

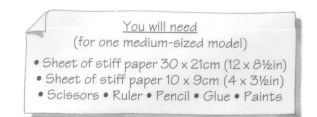

Making the house

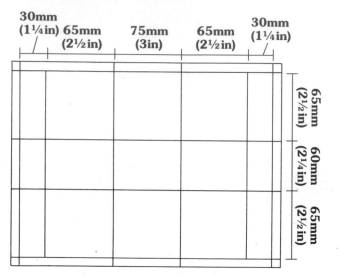

30mm (1¼in) 65mm (2½in) 75mm (3in) 65mm (2½in) 30mm (1¼in)

65mm (2½in) 60mm (2¼in) 65mm (2½in)

1. Measure and draw all the lines shown in the drawing above. Make sure you leave a border of about 1cm (½in) on all sides of the measurements, so you can make tabs (see step 2).

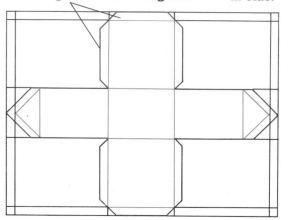

You'll use these tabs to hold the house together when it is glued.

Score all the lines shown in blue.

2. Draw tabs, about 1cm (½in) wide, onto your design. Then cut around the lines shown in red in the picture above, so you make the shape shown in step 3.

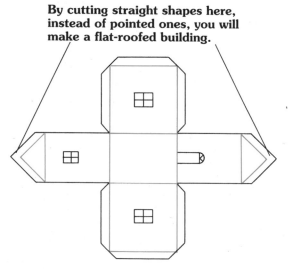

By cutting straight shapes here, instead of pointed ones, you will make a flat-roofed building.

3. Draw on doors, windows and any other details you want to show, then decorate the building in a style that you like. When you have done this, score all of the lines shown in blue in the picture above.

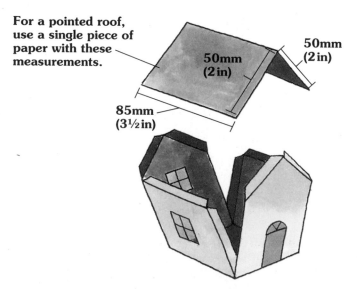

For a pointed roof, use a single piece of paper with these measurements.

50mm (2in)

50mm (2in)

85mm (3½in)

4. Fold the tabs in and put glue on them. Then fold the house together, pressing the tabs onto the shapes to make the parts hold together. Then add the roof. Make this according to the dimensions shown in the picture above.

Making the chimney

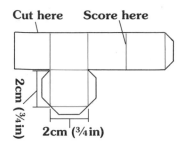

Cut here   Score here

2cm (¾ in)

2cm (¾ in)

Mark here

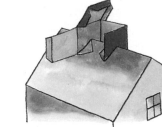

1. Copy the shapes shown above onto stiff paper. Carefully cut out the shapes and score the lines shown in blue.

2. Hold the chimney next to the roof and mark the shape on every other square. Cut the marks and fold the shapes.

3. Using the folded triangles as tabs, dab glue on them and fold the chimney around. Glue the paper into a box shape.

4. For a chimney pot, make a small tube. Cut and score one end to make tabs. Then bend them in and glue them to the chimney.

Decorating your houses

Decorate your houses in fine detail to make them as realistic as possible. If you like, you could make other things to place around the houses, such as model trees, or a street.

Authentic details add atmosphere. The roof of this Old English style house has been made to look like thatched straw.

Tall buildings can look imposing. This one has been decorated with lots of windows and heavy-looking columns around a large door to emphasize its grandness.

This house has been given French-style shutters. It has also been decorated so it looks like a house that has been converted into a bakery.

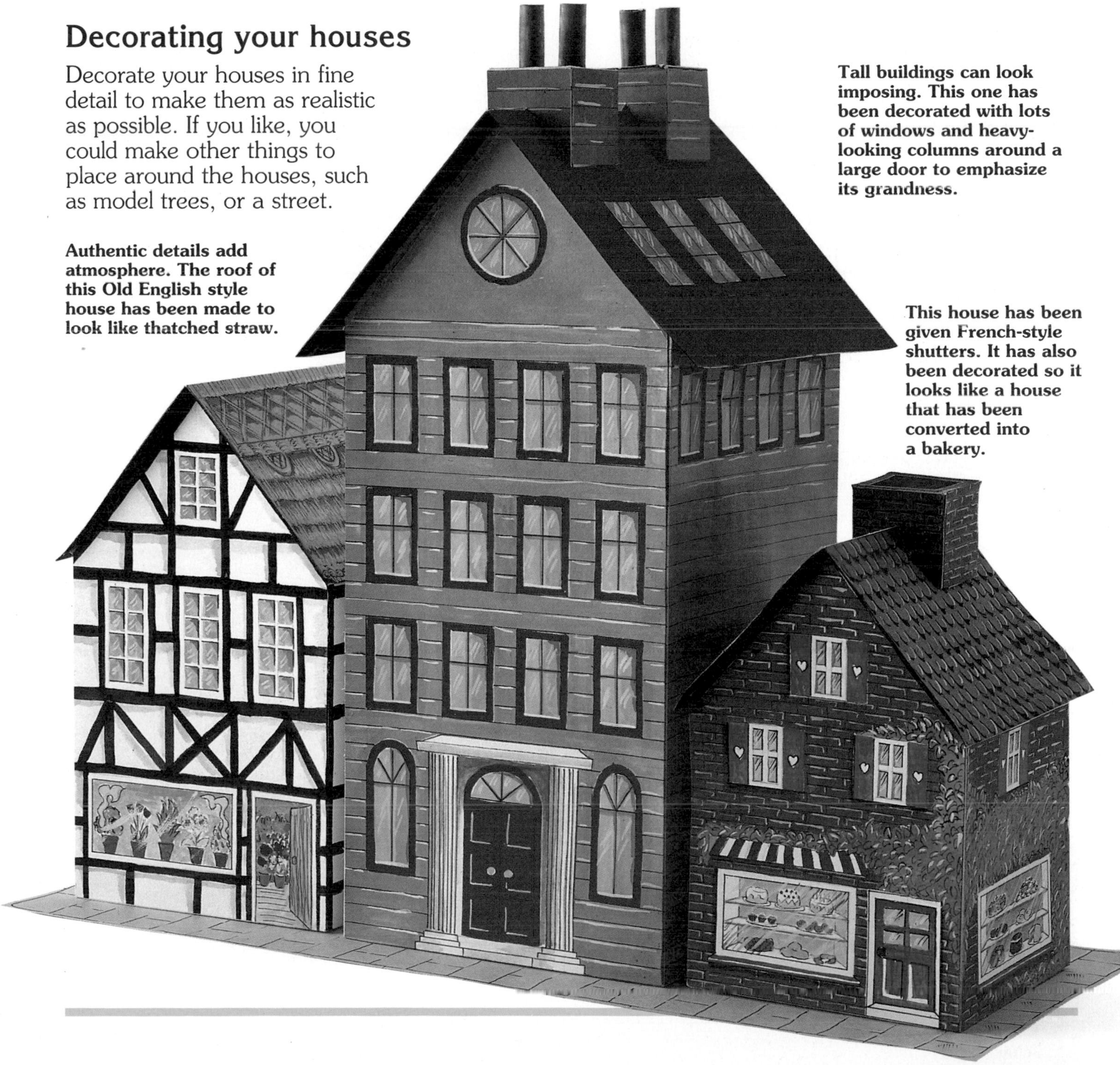

Papercraft safari

To make most of these stand-up animals, you simply cut out their shapes with their backs along a fold in a piece of paper. Make the deer first. By following its full instructions you will know how to make the other animals.*

Deer

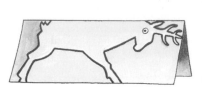

Score here.

Push down.

Push back.

1. Fold a piece of paper 20 x 16cm (8 x 6¼in) along its length. Trace the deer with its back and neck along the fold.

2. Cut out the shape carefully. Then open out the deer and score it along its neck, as shown above.

3. Fold back the head and neck along both of the scored lines. Then press along the fold so that the crease is sharp.

4. Fold the deer's body together again. Push the fold down into the body and push the neck back so that the head stands up. Then glue the head section together.

When you make the deer don't glue the antlers together. Instead, separate them so they stand apart.

Elephant

Fold a piece of paper in half along its longer sides. Then trace and cut out the elephant's body. Cut out two ears, two tusks and a tail separately from the body, following the shapes shown on page 91.

Glue the tail here.

Glue the ear tabs to the back of the elephant's head.

Fold each tusk at the tab.

Fold the tab here.

Ear tab

Glue the tusks here.

Tiger

Use a piece of orange-red paper. Fold it along its length and trace on the tiger's outline. Cut it out, then decorate it with markings similar to those shown in the photograph.

To make a leopard, draw a slimmer version of this cat. Decorate it yellow with black spots.

* Templates for all these animals are on pages 90-91.

Giraffe

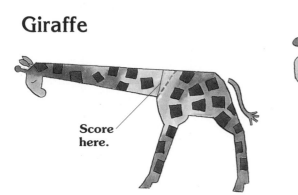

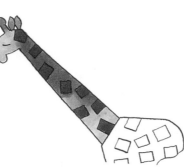

Score here.

1. Fold a piece of paper 30 x 20cm (12 x 8in) along its length. Trace and cut out the giraffe, then score the neck.

2. Fold along the line and bend the neck back so that it stands up at an angle from the body, just like a real giraffe's head.

It's best to use a deep yellow paper when making a giraffe. Add big orange-brown markings to the body.

To add eyes to your animals use white paint or crayon and black dots for pupils.

Glue the elephant's trunk together.

Glue a tongue to the snake's mouth.

To make a snake, trace the shape (on page 91) then decorate it as shown here and curl it around your fingers.

To make a snake, trace the shape (on page 91) then decorate it as shown here and curl it around your fingers.

Zebra

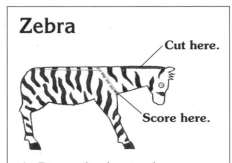

Cut here.

Score here.

1. Draw the basic shape onto a piece of folded white paper. On the neck make a score across and a cut along the top, as shown.

Mane shape

Tail

Glue the mane here.

2. Draw and cut out a fringed mane shape. Fill it in with black felt-tip and glue it between the neck halves. Add a black tail at the back. Then decorate the zebra with black stripes.

Crocodile puppet

This puppet has a body made from a strip of paper that is folded into a type of spring. On the finished puppet, the body twists and wriggles when you move the strings. The folding is fairly tricky until you get the knack, so follow the instructions closely.

Making the body

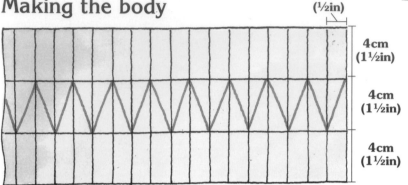

1.5cm (½in)

4cm (1½in)

4cm (1½in)

4cm (1½in)

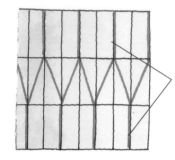

Score the lines all along the paper.

1. Using a pencil and ruler, draw lines onto the long piece of paper. You could use several lengths of paper together, to create a really long crocodile, if you like.

2. Score all the lines joining the points of the zig-zag to the edge of the paper. Then crease the lines firmly.

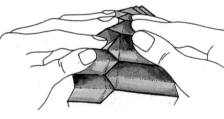

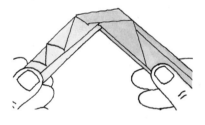

3. Turn the paper over. Score the lines between the creases. Then crease these lines.

4. Walk your fingers along the paper. Push the creases in and pinch the folds together.

5. Continue until all of the folds can be pinched between your fingers to make a shape like this.

Making the head and tail

Glue the back of the tongue to this part of the mouth.

Glue the teeth in here.

Tongue

Your folded crocodile head should look like this.

1. Fold the other piece of paper in half. Trace and cut out the head shape (the template is on page 92). Open and score the shapes as shown. Glue on a tongue and strips of paper teeth.

2. Now fold all the scored lines inward. Push in the crease between the V-shaped score at each side of the jaw so that the shape tucks inside the mouth. Add a tongue and decorate the head.

3. Glue some legs to the paper spring (see page 92). Then attach the head, using glue, and string up the crocodile with a needle and knotted thread as shown.

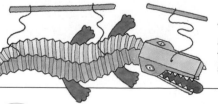

Tie the head string to a small stick. Tie the two back strings to a slightly longer stick.

Working the crocodile

Raise the head string to make the crocodile rear up. Jerk it to make the mouth open and close.

Rock the rear stick back and forth to make the crocodile hump its back as it moves along.

Bring the rear string around to the head, so the crocodile appears to chase its tail.

Glue the legs to the underside of the body so that the joins cannot be seen when you play with the finished crocodile.

Paper mobiles

Paper mobiles will move on the slightest breeze. They can be tricky to balance, but you can find out how to do this on page 88. Once you've made the ones shown here you could go on to invent designs of your own, showing sports stars or film stars, for instance.

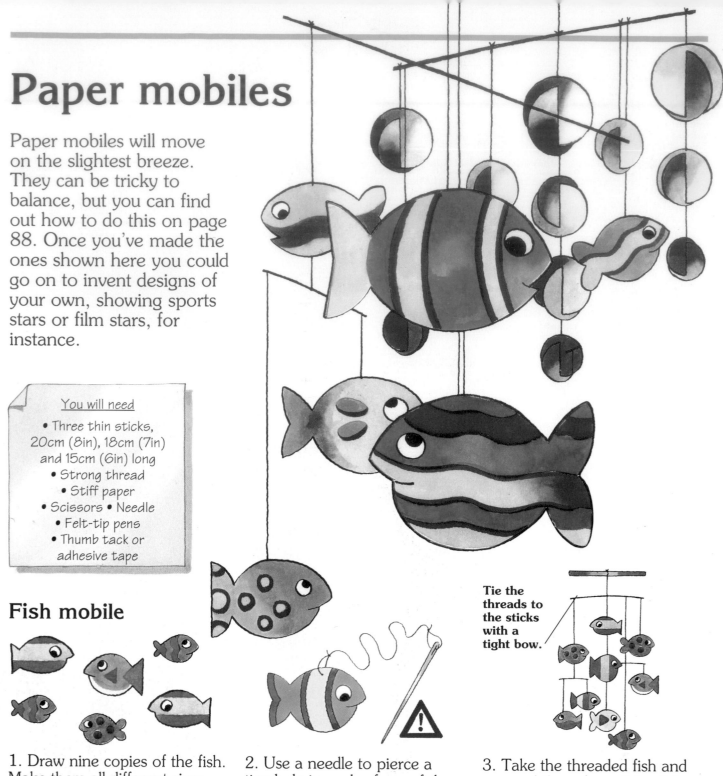

> ### You will need
> • Three thin sticks, 20cm (8in), 18cm (7in) and 15cm (6in) long
> • Strong thread
> • Stiff paper
> • Scissors • Needle
> • Felt-tip pens
> • Thumb tack or adhesive tape

Tie the threads to the sticks with a tight bow.

Fish mobile

1. Draw nine copies of the fish. Make them all different sizes. (You could photocopy* them at different sizes before you draw them.) Then decorate them using felt-tip pens.

2. Use a needle to pierce a tiny hole in each of your fish, near the top of its back. Then attach them to lengths of thread. Vary the length for each of the fish.

3. Take the threaded fish and suspend them from thin sticks, in the pattern shown above. Fix the finished mobile to the ceiling using a thumb tack or adhesive tape.

Ball mobile

You could make another mobile using circles slotted together, as shown here. Use paper that shines for a shimmering effect. You could go on to make a mobile using a combination of balls and fish.

Cut a slot halfway through each circle.

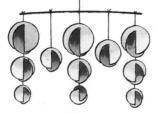

1. Cut out two paper circles for each ball. Then slot the two circles together.

2. Thread different-sized balls together and dangle them from a stick.

* Photocopiers are available for you to use at public libraries.

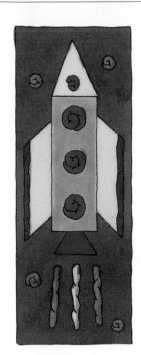

DECORATIVE THINGS

You will find lots of unusual, decorative things to make in this section. Amongst other projects there are beautiful paper flowers, stunning pictures and even an amazing-looking clock for you to make. You might like to use them to brighten up your room, or you could give them as gifts.

Useful technical tips are given on pages 86-87. The templates you will need in this section are on page 93.

⚠️

To avoid injury, be careful when you see a warning triangle.

Handy decorations

The handy decorations on this page will make eye-catching bookmarks, especially if you decorate them using bright felt-tips. The place mats on the opposite page are great for brightening up mealtimes.

Hand bookmark

1. Draw around your hand with a black felt-tip. If you make any mistakes on the outline, you can cut them out later.

2. Decorate the hand shape brightly. You could follow the idea shown here or invent a design of your own.

3. Cut out the finished picture carefully. At this point, trim off any untidy felt-tip marks from the outline.

4. Glue the hand shape onto the top of a strip of paper. Place the finished shape in a book, with the fingers sticking out of the top.

Wiggly worm bookmarks

Draw, decorate and cut out worm shapes, just like the ones below. They should be longer than the height of a book so that their heads and tails will stick out at top and bottom.

Give your worm some clothes, or draw on things like glasses or a bow tie.

Mosaic place mat

You will need
- Large piece of cardboard, such as from an empty cereal box • Scissors
- Pictures from an old magazine
- Plastic food wrap • Felt-tip pens

Make sure the pictures you use are not wanted by anybody else before you tear them up.

1. Cut a large rectangle from the cardboard, about 30 x 20cm (12 x 8in). Round off the corners using scissors.

2. Using a felt-tip pen, draw a big, bold design. Include clear features, which will be easy to pick out and decorate.

3. Tear the magazine pictures into small squares. Split up the pieces, so that all red pieces are together, and so on.

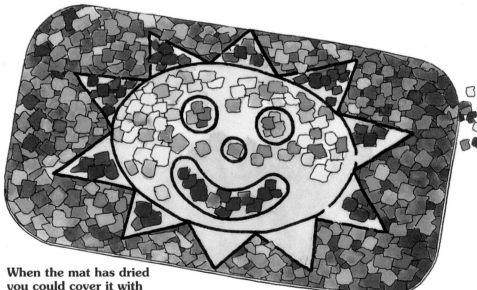

When the mat has dried you could cover it with plastic food wrap, taped on at the back.

4. Stick the pieces onto the design, so that you create big, bold blocks of tone in different parts of the picture. Overlap the pieces to create stronger tones. You may need to use lots of paper, so be sure to tear up plenty before you start.

Extra ideas

Here are some more designs for attractive place mats. You might like to copy these and decorate them with pieces of paper. Alternatively, you could make mats using designs of your own, based on things that you like.

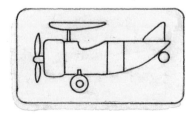

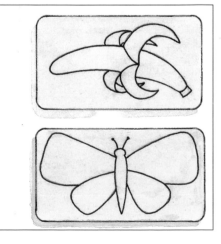

Paper flowers

These paper flowers can make great decorations for any room. To make them you will need crêpe paper and garden wire. You can buy crêpe paper at artists' suppliers. Garden wire is available from gardening stores.

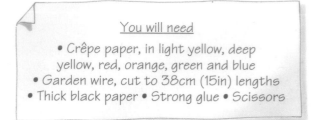
Daffodils

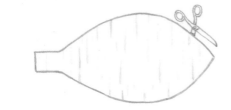

1. To make the trumpet, cut out a rectangle 2 x 5cm (¾ x 2in) and stretch one of the long edges to make it frilled.

2. Roll the paper into a tube and glue it. Twist the bottom around the end of a wire and glue it on.

3. To make the petals, cut out six shapes similar to the shape above, from yellow crêpe paper.

Bend the stem near the flower head, to make it face forward.

4. Stretch the petals in the way the arrows show. Then fold them in half to make a crease down the middle.

5. Open the petals out. Put a dot of glue around the base of the trumpet. Glue the petals around it one by one.

6. Fan out the petals. Glue a strip of green paper around the flower base, then wind it down the stem and glue it.

You could tie your flowers with a bow made from crêpe paper or a ribbon, to make them into a bouquet.

Poppies

 **Use thick black paper for this.**

1. Make a middle for the flower by cutting out a piece of black paper to the size shown here. Make cuts all along it, as shown.

2. Spread glue along one end of the black paper and wind it tightly around the end of a wire stem. Then glue the other end to hold it in place.

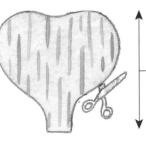

The crinkles in the paper should run in this direction.

3. Following the shape shown above, cut eight petals out of crêpe paper. Cut them so that the crinkles in the paper are running up and down.

For maximum effect you could arrange your flowers in a vase with sprigs of green leaf, made from crêpe paper.

 **Hold the petals like this to stretch them.**

4. Shape the petals by stretching them out from the middle a little. Then glue them around the middle piece of paper.

5. Glue a long strip of green crêpe paper to the bottom of the flower. Wind it down the wire and glue the end in place.

3-D pictures

By following the instructions on these two pages you can create paper pictures that stand away from their backgrounds. Using rolled-up, painted toilet tissue, you can make all kinds of imaginative designs. There are suggestions on the opposite page – or you can use ideas of your own.

Making a flower picture

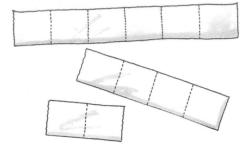

1. Place a small plate half onto a piece of pale paper. Draw around the rim of the plate and cut out the shape.

2. Paint a pattern on the bowl shape and leave it to dry. You might like to copy the pattern from a real bowl that you have.

3. Tear six-sheet, four-sheet and two-sheet lengths of white toilet tissue. You will need about 18 lengths in all.

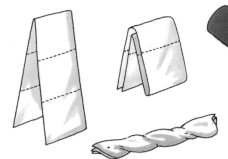

You can dip the twists into two different paints for an interesting effect.

4. To make the flowers, fold the six- and four-sheet lengths of paper in half and then in half again. Twist them lightly into rolls, as shown.

5. Pour paint onto four plates, using one plate for each paint. Mix a little water into the paint and then spread it around with a teaspoon, to make it runny.

6. Roll the paper twists lightly in the paint. Then dip them quickly into a bowl of warm water and allow them to drip for a few seconds.

Bring the two ends together.

Pinch the paper at each end to make a leaf shape.

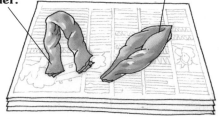

7. Coil the twists onto a thick pad of newspaper. Press the paper lightly so that a little water seeps out and the paint runs.

8. For leaves, fold the two-sheet lengths before twisting. Dip them in green paint and then water. Shape them, as above.

9. Lay the flowers and leaves on a baking tray. Then heat them at a low oven setting until they are dry.

10. Glue the bowl shape onto black paper. Arrange the flowers with the largest in the middle, filling in the gaps with leaves and smaller flowers. Glue them in place and let the glue dry. Then you can hang up your work to decorate a wall.

Other ideas

Here are some alternative subjects for your 3-D pictures, using the basic rolled-up pieces of toilet tissue.

Lady with a hat

Family of snails

Blossom tree

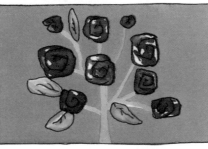

Besides making circular shapes with your toilet tissue, you could make long shapes to decorate your pictures. Two examples are shown on the right, but there are lots of other subjects you could choose.

Space rocket

Tropical fish

Sunflower

Real sunflowers are big and striking. You can make paper models of them that are every bit as eye-catching as the real things. For the best effect, tape your finished sunflower inside a window.

You will need
- Round plastic lid from a margarine tub
- Brown paint
- Paintbrush
- Scissors
- Green and yellow crêpe paper
- Wrapping paper
- Glue
- Double-sided adhesive tape
- Adhesive tape
- Tracing paper
- Pencil
- Paper clips

1. Mix some brown paint with a little glue. Paint roughly around the edges of the top of the margarine tub's lid, and down the sides. Let it dry.

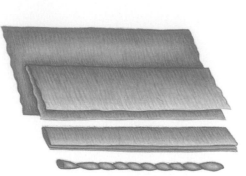

2. Cut three strips of yellow crêpe paper, 30 x 10cm (12 x 4in). Fold the long sides together twice and crease. Twist each tightly into a rope.

Brown paint will shade the ridges and creases.

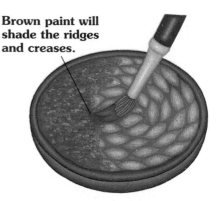

3. Paint the top of the lid with lots of glue. Wind the end of one rope around on itself into a flat spiral. Press this onto the middle of the lid.

Press the ropes down firmly.

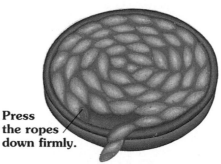

4. Keep winding the rope around itself and pressing it onto the lid. Where it ends, start with another rope, until the lid is full.

5. Dip a paintbrush in the brown paint. Wipe it on some newspaper until it is almost dry. Brush it all over your spiral then leave it to dry.

Hold layers of paper together with paper clips.

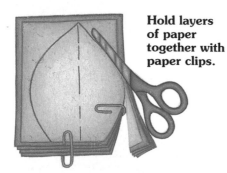

6. Trace the petal template on page 92. Cut it out and paper clip it to a piece of crêpe paper, 16 x 10cm (6¼ x 4in). Cut out 16 petals. You can cut several layers at once.

7. Turn the lid face-down and spread glue all around the edge. Pull the petal out at its widest part and then fold a pleat in it carefully, as shown in the picture above.

Make sure the pleat stays in the petal when you glue it onto the lid.

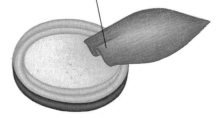

8. Turn the petal over and stick it to the glued edge of the lid. Do the same with more petals and glue them all around the lid side by side. Don't overlap them.

Back view

9. For a second layer, don't stretch or pleat the petals. Put glue on the bottom edge, then press them on in between the others. They will overlap.

10. Fold and twist a long rope of green crêpe paper 25cm (10in) wide, as in step 2. Curve it, then tape it on a window using some double-sided adhesive tape. Finally, attach the flower's large head.

Copy this shape for the flower pot.

11. Trace the leaf template on page 92. Cut three green crêpe leaves. Attach them on alternate sides of the stem. Cut out a flower pot shape from wrapping paper. Tape it over the stem.

Position the bottom of the pot at the bottom of a window pane.

You could tape your sunflower on a wall, if you like.

Papier mâché cactus

Using a few long balloons and an assortment of paper you can make a model cactus. The project will take a few days to complete, but it is well worth it. You could make your finished cactus into the main attraction of a desert scene, complete with sand and an empty water bottle.

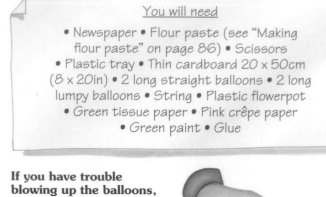

If you have trouble blowing up the balloons, you could ask an adult to do it for you.

1. Make some flour paste according to the recipe on page 86. You'll need to boil the mixture, so you may want an adult to help you.

2. Stretch the straight balloons with your fingers, or by filling them with water and emptying them. Then blow them up and fasten their ends.

Tape the cardboard in a roll around the balloons.

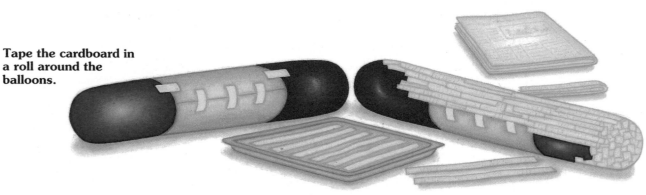

3. Tie the fastened ends together with string. Roll the thin cardboard around where the balloons join and tape it.

4. Cut newspaper strips about 10 x 30cm (4 x 12in). Lay lots of strips on a plastic tray and cover them with flour paste.

5. Paste strips lengthways all over the balloons, from the middle out. Cover one end with squares of pasted newspaper.

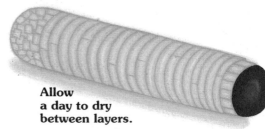

Allow a day to dry between layers.

Put pebbles on top of the paper.

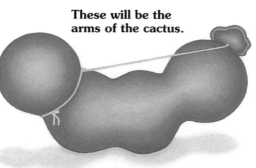

These will be the arms of the cactus.

6. Do a second layer with strips going the other way. Leave them in a warm place to dry. Do three more layers in alternate directions.

7. When dry, trim the ends with scissors. The balloons will go down gently. Wedge the shape into the flower pot with newspaper.

8. Blow up both lumpy balloons. Tie a long string around the end of each. Pull the string to bend the balloon and tie it around the last bump.

Paste more strips over the end of the string.

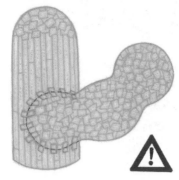

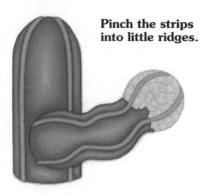

Pinch the strips into little ridges.

9. Paste on three layers of newspaper. Use 10 x 10cm (4 x 4in) squares. Leave the paper to dry between layers. Cut off the string.

10. Cut circles in the stem to push the arms in. Make small holes first and enlarge them if necessary. Paste strips over the joins.

11. Paste, then roll and twist, 15cm (6in) strips of green tissue paper. Add to the cactus in stripes. Paint green between the stripes.

The finished cactus stands about 1m (3ft) high.

A real cactus of this type could grow to a height of over 15m (50ft).

Making flowers

Cut a strip of pink crêpe 9cm (3½in) wide. Make deep points in one side.

Wind and gather the straight edge into a roll and tie it with thread.

Cut a cross shape into the top of each arm. Push the flowers into them.

If you haven't any sand, use small pebbles instead.

Papier mâché plate

Papier mâché plates can make great decorations. Before you begin, you will need to make some paper pulp, following the instructions on page 86. You can form the pulp into the shapes of animals and paint them with bright paints to create striking effects. Use paste to stick the layers of paper together (the details for how to make paste are also on page 86).

following the instructions on page 86

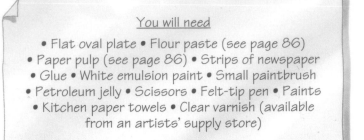
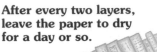

You will need
- Flat oval plate • Flour paste (see page 86)
- Paper pulp (see page 86) • Strips of newspaper
- Glue • White emulsion paint • Small paintbrush
- Petroleum jelly • Scissors • Felt-tip pen • Paints
- Kitchen paper towels • Clear varnish (available from an artists' supply store)

Tiger plate

Let the strips of newspaper stick out over the edge.

After every two layers, leave the paper to dry for a day or so.

1. Using your fingers, smear the top surface of the plate with a very thin layer of petroleum jelly.

2. Paste a layer of strips across the plate. Use shorter strips on curved parts. Make sure you cover the top of the plate.

3. Smooth paste on the first layer with your fingers and paste a second layer on the other way. Leave it to dry.

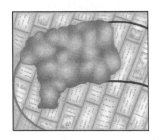
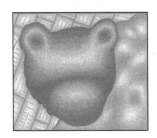

4. Build up about eight layers of paper. When they are dry draw a design onto the plate, using felt-tip.

5. Roll and flatten balls of soaked paper within the outline to make a raised shape. Build up the shape gradually.

6. When the body is dry build up the head. Make a round shape and add small lumps for the chin and ears.

Don't take the paper off too soon or it will buckle.

Tissue paper gives the plate a smooth finish.

7. After a couple of days, when it is completely dry, ease the paper off the dish. Trim the edge with scissors.

8. Wipe off all the petroleum jelly with kitchen paper towels. Glue strips over the edges and leave them to dry.

9. Paste on two layers of tissue paper. When it is dry, paint the plate white. Decorate the plate as shown in the photograph.

Paint the main blocks first. When they are dry, add the small details and patterns.

When everything is dry, add two or three layers of clear varnish.

The shape of this cat, with its back arched, complements the roundness of the plate.

Extra ideas

These plates all show animals, but you could show people or even machines on your plates. Whatever you do, make sure that the shape of thing you show matches the shape of the plate.

Another cat. This one has a more arched back, to suit the type of plate it is on.

This plate has a checked tablecloth background with a lobster on it.

This dish shows a snake protecting its eggs.

Papercraft clock

To make the beautiful clock shown here you will need to buy a clock mechanism. They aren't expensive – you can get them from craft stores. Alternatively, you could buy a cheap clock and take it apart. This project is a little tricky so follow the instructions closely.

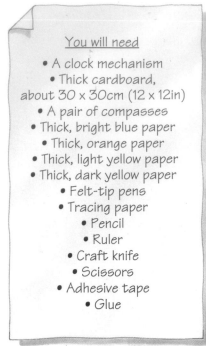
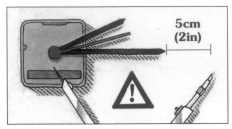

1. Open a pair of compasses so that they are 5cm (2in) wider than the long hand of the clock. Draw a circle on the thick cardboard. Cut out the circle using a craft knife.

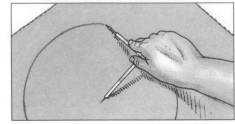

2. Draw a circle the same size as the cardboard onto the dark yellow paper and onto a piece of tracing paper. Use scissors to cut out both of these new shapes.

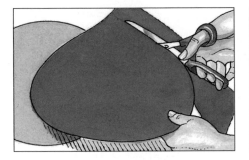

3. Reduce the width of the pair of compasses by about 1cm (½in). Then use them to draw a circle on the blue paper. Cut out the circle using scissors.

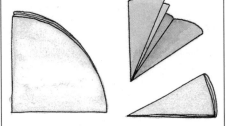

4. Fold the tracing paper into quarters. Then fold it into thirds by bending both edges in so that they overlap. Crease the folds, so the shapes stay folded.

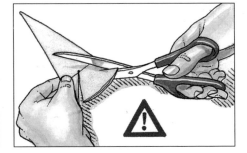

5. Draw a line 4cm (1½in) from the outside edge of the folded tracing paper. Make a mark halfway along this line. Cut in from both corners to this mark, as shown above.

6. Open out the tracing paper and spread it on the pale yellow paper. Draw around it carefully, then use a ruler to straighten the lines. Cut out the star shape.

7. Set the compasses to 1cm (½in) wider than the short hand of your clock. Draw a circle on the dark yellow paper. Cut it out and put it in the middle of the star. Draw around it.

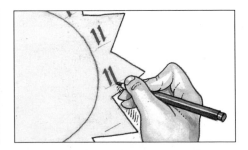

8. Draw each number onto one of the points. Either draw them freehand, or trace them from the shapes on page 93 and transfer them onto the clock.

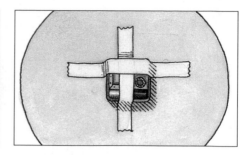

9. Glue the circles and the star to the cardboard, starting with the biggest one. Now decorate the face (see below). Enlarge the central hole with some scissors.

10. Take the hands off the clock mechanism. Push the spindle of the mechanism through the hole from the back. Replace the hands on the front of the clock.

11. Attach the mechanism to the back of the clock with masking tape. If you want to make your clock more hard wearing, you could cover it with clear, adhesive-backed plastic*.

Decorating the face

Make the face after attaching the circles and star in step 9. Begin by cutting an orange circle, the same size as the dark yellow one.

1. Draw the features marked by the blue lines. Then cut them out.

2. Glue the face and left eye onto the yellow circle.

3. Turn over the lips and cheek. Glue them into place.

Hang the clock on a wall by taping string to the back.

* Adhesive-backed plastic is available from craft stores and artists' supply stores.

Paper bowl

This type of paper bowl is a great way to recycle old newspapers or cardboard egg cartons. Each one will take about 45 minutes to make, and about an hour to dry if you leave it in an oven set to a low temperature.

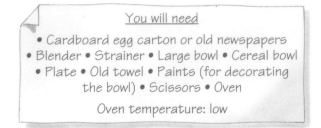

You will need
- Cardboard egg carton or old newspapers
- Blender • Strainer • Large bowl • Cereal bowl
- Plate • Old towel • Paints (for decorating the bowl) • Scissors • Oven

Oven temperature: low

Making the bowl

If you don't have a blender, squash the pieces up with your hands.

1. Tear the egg carton (or newspaper) into pieces and soak them in warm water in a large bowl until they are soft (about 10–20 minutes).

2. Pour some of the water into the blender. Switch it on and add the soft, mushy pieces gradually until you have made a watery pulp.

3. Pour the mixture into a fine-mesh strainer over the sink. Gradually press down on the pulp to squeeze out most of the water.

Cover the bowl completely.

4. Place the upturned cereal bowl onto a plate. Cover it with plastic food wrap. Then press small lumps of paper pulp all over it, until you have built up a thickness of around 2cm (¾in).

5. Place the towel over the bowl and press it firmly all over, to flatten the pulp and remove the excess water. Wring out the towel if it becomes waterlogged.

6. Set an oven to a low temperature. Leave the bowl in it for an hour or so, until it is completely dry. Take care that you don't burn the bowl when you do this.

You could decorate the bowl using paints, in a style that is in keeping with the things that you're going to put in it.

7. When the pulp has dried, remove it from the cereal bowl and trim around the edge with scissors.

For a stronger bowl, you could knead a little non-fungicidal wallpaper paste into the pulp after you have strained it.

GREETING CARDS AND GIFT PACKINGS

This section contains guides to making greeting cards that you could use for all sorts of occasions. There are also instructions showing how to make really attractive boxes and decorated paper, which you could use for wrapping gifts.

Useful extra tips for this section can be found on pages 86-87.

Techniques that could be dangerous have a warning triangle next to them. Take care when you see these.

Quick cards

These cards are quick and easy to make and although they are simple they will look really striking. You can adapt the ideas by using all sorts of decorations to make a range of different cards.

You will need
- Stiff paper in a variety of shades at least 30 x 20 cm (12 x 8in)
- Felt-tip pens or crayons • Ruler
- Scissors • Glue

Simple pop-ups

Press firmly along the folds to make a crease.

Put glue on this side.

1. Cut an oblong piece of paper 30 x 20cm (12 x 8in) and fold it in half along its longer sides.

2. Cut a paper strip about 3cm (1in) wide and half the length of the first piece. Fold its longest sides in half.

3. Open it out, turn it over, and fold each end up about 1cm (½in), to make tabs. Then put glue onto each end.

Lift the top half of the big piece toward you so that the small piece stands out.

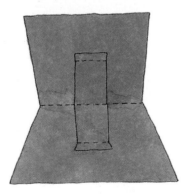

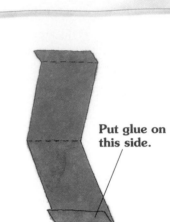

When you open the card the picture will pop up.

4. Lay the small piece down the middle of the larger piece, glue-side down, so that the crease of the small piece lies inside the crease of the larger piece of card.

5. Decorate and cut out a picture to cover the lower half of the small piece. Put some glue on its lower part and then press it in place.

More ideas

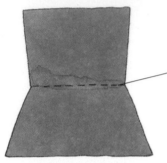

You could copy these designs and use them in your pop-up cards. Decorate them so that they go with the shade of cardboard you use.

Write your message here.

Contrast cards

You will need
- Stiff paper in contrasting shades, at least 30 x 20cm (12 x 8in)
- Scissors
- Glue

These cards will look really striking if you design them with strong, simple shapes and patterns.

1. Fold an oblong piece of paper 30 x 20cm (12 x 8in) in half along its longer edges to make a greeting card shape.

2. Using a contrasting shade of paper, cut another piece, half the width of the front of the first piece.

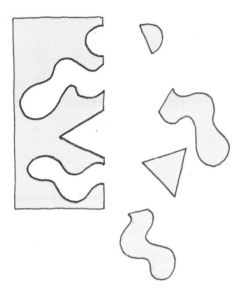

3. Using scissors, cut deep shapes starting from the right hand side. Save all the pieces that you cut.

4. Stick the second piece of cardboard, with pieces cut out, to the left-hand edge of the front of the folded card.

5. Turn over the cut-out pieces and stick them down opposite the corresponding shapes, so they mirror each other.

Other ideas

A pine tree makes a good contrast card because it is the same on both sides. Houses also make a good shape.

Photo cards

1. Cut some faces of your family from unwanted old photos. They can be quite small.

2. Stick faces onto a card, then draw a picture around them.

Assorted greetings

You can use all sorts of simple ideas to make different types of pop-up cards. The assortment shown here can be made in any size you like. For really big versions use stiff cardboard, as this will stand up more easily than paper.

Stand-up cards

Make the hole at the edge of the picture.

1. Mark a line halfway down a piece of thin cardboard. Draw a picture on it.

2. Push the point of a pencil into the card above the line, to make a small hole.

3. Carefully push one scissor blade into the hole. Cut around the shape above the line.

4. Fold the card back firmly along the line to make the picture stand up.

Genie in a jar

1. Take an empty plastic jar with a screw-on lid. Mix some paint with water and glue. Paint it on the inside of the jar.

2. Cut a strip of cardboard three times the height of the jar. Make narrow folds all along it, at 1cm (½in) intervals. Cut out and decorate a genie, like the one on the right. Glue it to the top of the folded strip. Stick a feather and thread to the genie's turban.

When you take off the lid the genie will pop out.

3. Glue the bottom of the folded strip inside the jar. Tape the end of the thread to the jar lid and screw it on.

Flapping wings

Fold both ways.

1. Draw two curved lines onto a piece of folded paper. Cut part of each line. Then fold along the rest.

2. Open the paper and pull the wings toward you. Stick the paper onto a piece of cardboard the same size using glue.

3. Draw a bee's body in-between the wings. When you open and close the card you will make the wings flap.

By cutting a single flap, you could make a newspaper or a book. Complete the design by drawing a reader.

Spring card

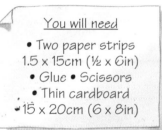
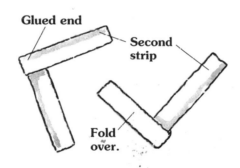

Glued end

Second strip

Fold over.

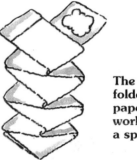

The folded paper works as a spring.

You could design your own versions of this card, featuring a frog, for example.

1. Glue the end of one of the two paper strips. Press the second strip on the glued end at right angles. Fold the strips over each other until all paper is used.

2. Dab some glue under the top flap, then press down firmly. Cut off any extra paper to leave a folded paper spring.

Completing the card

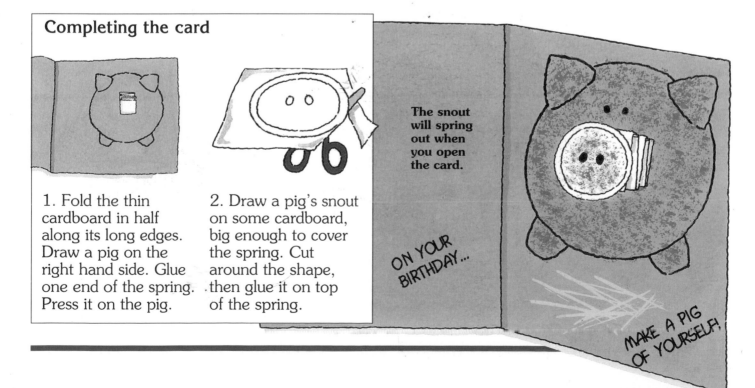

The snout will spring out when you open the card.

1. Fold the thin cardboard in half along its long edges. Draw a pig on the right hand side. Glue one end of the spring. Press it on the pig.

2. Draw a pig's snout on some cardboard, big enough to cover the spring. Cut around the shape, then glue it on top of the spring.

ON YOUR BIRTHDAY...

MAKE A PIG OF YOURSELF!

Dancing snowmen card

This pop-up design makes a great card to send in winter. You could use the basic design to create all sorts of cards, but make sure that you choose simple shapes that will work well when they are connected in a row, such as star shapes.

You will need
• White paper 13 x 30cm (5 x 12in)
• White paper 4 x 30cm (1½ x 12in)
• Black card 16 x 30cm (6 x 12in)
• Pencil • Eraser • Scissors • Glue
• Pencil crayons • Felt-tips

Making the card

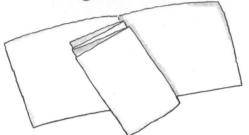

The arms must touch the sides of the paper.

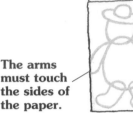

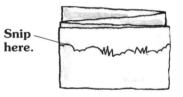

1. Fold a piece of white paper, 13 x 30cm (5 x 12in) along its longest edges. Open out the paper, then fold it back so that it makes the shape shown above.

2. Keeping the paper folded, lightly draw a circle for a snowman's head, using a pencil. Then draw an oval for the body and add arms, legs and a hat.

3. To strengthen the snowman's outline, go over it with a pencil crayon or a felt-tip. Then rub out all the other pencil lines, to neaten the shapes.

You could draw stars in pencil on the snowman to remind yourself not to cut here.

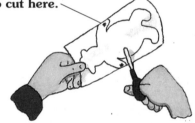

Make sure that the pencil outlines don't show.

This piece will become the snow-covered ground on the finished card.

Snip here.

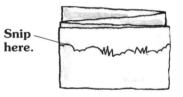

4. Cut around the outline. Keep the paper folded. Be careful not to cut around the ends of the snowman's arms.

5. Carefully open out the snowmen. Add faces, scarves and so on. You could make each one different.

6. Cut a strip of white paper, 4 x 30cm (1½ x 12in). Fold it as shown in step 1. Then snip bumpy shapes out of the top.

Attaching the snowmen

1. Fold a piece of black card, 16 x 30cm (6 x 12in). Put some glue on the backs of the first and last snowmen.

2. Lay the middle fold of the snowmen along the card's middle. Lay them fairly near to the top of the card.

3. Press down the snowmen. Pull the middle two to you and close the card. When you open the card, they will stand out.

You could paint some falling snow on the background.

Glue the snowy ground to the card in the same way that you attached the snowmen. Leave a space between the snowmen and the lawn.

You could base your snowmen on people that you know.

Other ideas

Here are two other ideas that you could copy.

Pop-up cakes with presents in the background will make an ideal birthday card.

Almost any sort of flower will look great on this type of card.

Quick paper boxes

These boxes are great for packing small presents in. You make them using origami paper folds. There are origami tips on page 87.

There are origami tips on page 87.

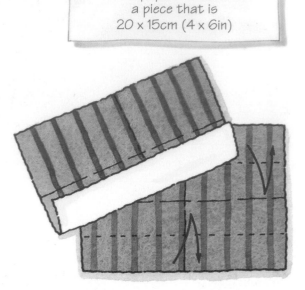

Making the boxes

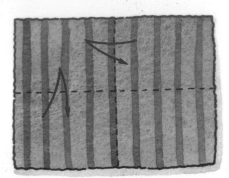

1. Fold a piece of paper 20 x 15cm (4 x 6in) along its smaller sides and unfold it. Then fold it along its longer sides and unfold it.

2. Keeping the paper on the table, fold both the long edges into the middle crease. Then unfold them.

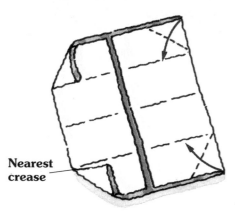

Nearest crease

3. Fold both the short edges into the middle crease. Leave them there while you do the next stage.

4. Fold in all the corners so that they meet the nearest crease that goes across the paper, as shown above.

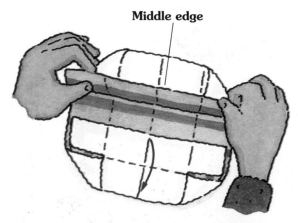

Middle edge

5. Fold back the edges from the middle so that they cover the corners.

6. Now put a finger inside each corner and pull them out gently.

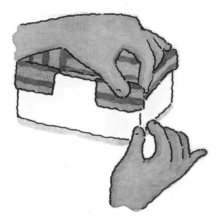

7. Finally, turn the box over. Pinch the corners and smooth along the sides to make it stand upright.

You could try making the boxes in different shapes and sizes.

For a long thin box you need to fold these edges back twice.

Other ideas

Gift boxes

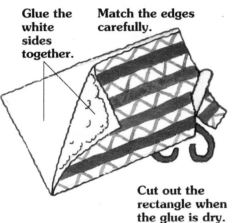

Glue the white sides together.

Match the edges carefully.

Cut out the rectangle when the glue is dry.

1. Stick two pieces of decorated paper together. Allow the paper to dry before you start folding it.

Pack the box neatly to make an impressive display.

Wrap it carefully, so the gift is as attractive as possible.

2. Pack your box with a face cloth, soap and bath pearls. Then wrap it in cling film and tie on a ribbon. You could add a paper flower for decoration (see page 27).

Box nest

12 x 18cm (4 x 7in)

10 x 16cm (3 x 6in)

14 x 20cm (5 x 8in)

Prepare several paper rectangles. Make the sides of each one 2cm (¾in) smaller than the one before. You could give this collection of boxes away as a gift in itself.

Paper sizes

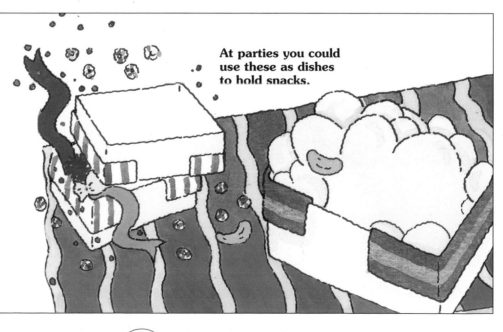

• Your boxes will be half the size of the rectangles you start with. For example, for a 6 x 12cm (2 x 5in) box, start with a 12 x 24cm (4 x 10in) rectangle of paper.

• You will always need to use rectangles of paper for these boxes. You cannot make them from squares.

• To use as a lid, make a slightly larger box.

At parties you could use these as dishes to hold snacks.

Pop-out greeting cards

You can make cards with parts that pop-out at you when you open them, like those on the opposite page. All of the cards shown are made in the same way but are adapted and decorated differently. You could adapt this idea, using your own designs.

You will need
• Thin cardboard 20 x 28cm (8 x 11in)
• Two pieces of white paper 20 x 28cm (8 x 11in) • Ruler • Scissors
• Pencil • Pencil crayons or felt-tips

Making the pop-out piece

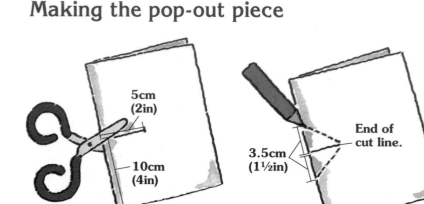

5cm (2in)

10cm (4in)

3.5cm (1½in)

End of cut line.

Fold along the pencil line.

Flap

Repeat this stage on both sides of the folded card.

1. Fold one of the paper pieces in half along its long edges. Then mark 10cm (4in) up the folded edge of the paper with a pencil. Draw a 5cm (2in) line from the mark and cut it.

2. Using a pencil, make a mark 3.5cm (1½in) above and below the cut line, on the folded edge of the paper. Draw a line from each mark to the other end of the cut.

3. Fold back two flaps. Then open them out and turn the paper over. On the other side fold the flaps down and then open them out once again.

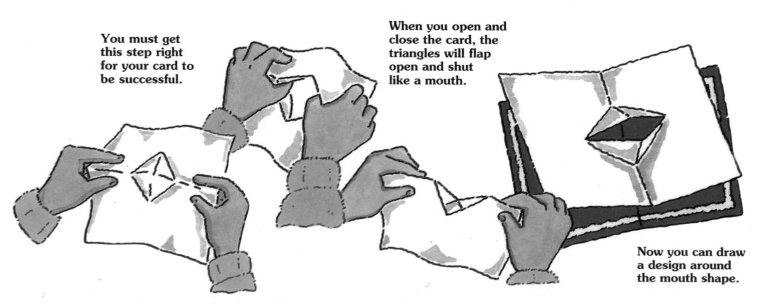

You must get this step right for your card to be successful.

When you open and close the card, the triangles will flap open and shut like a mouth.

Now you can draw a design around the mouth shape.

4. Lay the paper out flat. Pinch up the folds at each end of the paper. They will change so that the folds stick out.

5. Pinch the folded triangle shapes and push them through to the other side. Press the card to flatten the triangles inside.

6. Fold the cardboard in the same way as the paper in step 1. Lay the paper on top, matching the middle folds.

Other ideas

If you'd like to try drawing a new pop-out card you could make your own versions of the subjects shown here. As you can see, you don't have to make them so they open out sideways.

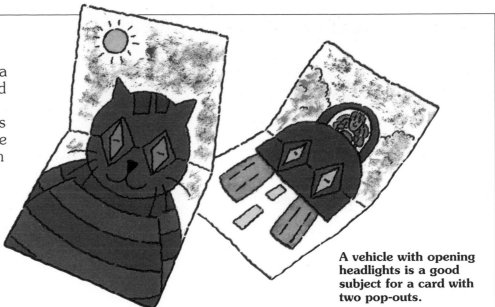

Two pop-outs can be used to make eyes that become wider and narrower as you open and close the card.

A vehicle with opening headlights is a good subject for a card with two pop-outs.

Backgrounds

Both the cards shown here have detailed backgrounds. Plan your backgrounds before you begin drawing around the pop-out part of the card. Draw them so they are clear and strong looking, but not so full of detail that they are hard to see. Also, make sure the pop-out part of the card stands out well, so that it has maximum impact.

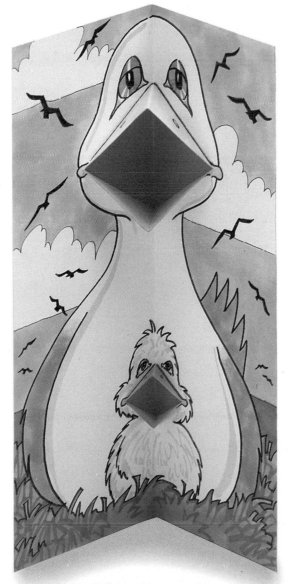

This card uses two pop-out shapes instead of one. It is fairly easy to make – simply cut an extra pop-out piece when you begin.

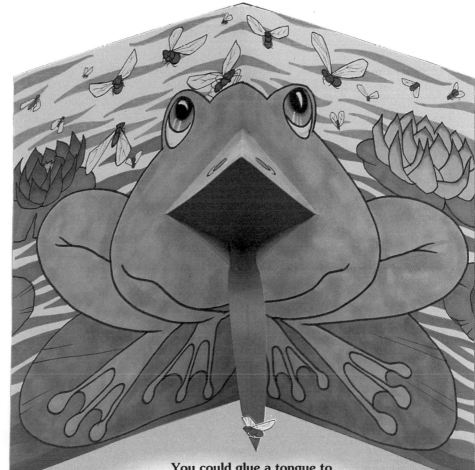

You could glue a tongue to the lower jaw so it pops out when you open the card.

Print your own paper

You can make a dazzling selection of hand-printed papers using things such as oil paints, turpentine, cardboard, ink and potatoes. Use your paper to wrap presents, or give it to friends as a gift in itself.

Making marbled paper

1. Put blobs of oil paint (which you can buy from artists' supply stores) on a plate. Mix a few drops of turpentine into it with a knife to make it runny.

2. Pour a little water into a bowl. The bowl must be at least as big as your paper. A washing bowl will probably be big enough.

3. Dip the knife in the paint and shake it onto the water. Swirl it around gently. The more you swirl the paint, the smaller your pattern will be.

4. Gently lay your paper on top of the water, then lift it off again. Leave the paper to dry on some old newspaper.

5. Clean the plate, knife and bowl with turpentine. Then wash them in hot soapy water, to remove the turpentine.

Potato prints

You will need
- A large potato • Paint
- Paper • Knife
- Old plate

Don't forget that your print will be back to front.

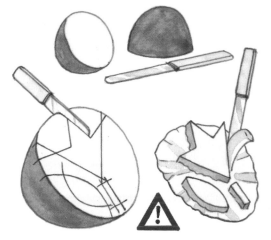

1. Cut a large potato in half. Cut a shape on the flat side, then cut away the potato so that the shape stands out.

2. Mix some paint with a little water on a plate. Press the cut side of the potato into it, so it becomes covered in the paint.

3. Press the potato onto the paper to make a print. Make more prints all over the paper to make a pattern.

Stencils

You will need
- Thin cardboard • Scissors
- Pencil • Old toothbrush
- Paint • Paper

You could make all sorts of designs, including the fish and trees shown here.

1. Draw a shape on some thin cardboard. Push the point of your scissors into it. Cut it out to make a stencil.

2. Place the stencil on some paper. Dip an old toothbrush in paint. Hold it over the stencil and stroke the bristles.

3. Spatter the paint evenly over the stencil. Lift off the stencil and do the same again until the pattern is all over the paper.

Origami star boxes

You could use this type of box to hold little things, such as buttons and beads. For the best results make the boxes from wrapping paper, or paper that you have decorated yourself. This project is tricky, so you might like to ask an adult to help you.*

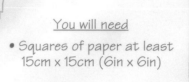

You will need
• Squares of paper at least 15cm x 15cm (6in x 6in)

Starting the box

1. Take a square of paper, decorated side up. Make two creases by folding the opposite corners together.

2. Turn the paper over. Make two more creases by folding the paper in half from side to side and from bottom to top.

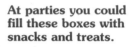

At parties you could fill these boxes with snacks and treats.

3. Leave the paper folded in half from bottom to top and hold it along the fold.

4. Gently bring your fingers together so that all the corners meet in the middle.

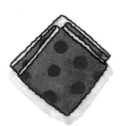

5. Fold the flap in front to the right and the flap behind to the left.

6. Flatten the paper to complete the shape. Check that two flaps are on each side.

* For extra information on origami, see page 87.

Completing the box

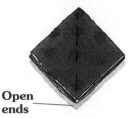

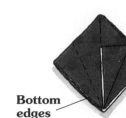

Open ends

Leave this flap on the table.

Bottom edges

Press here to open.

1. Turn the folded square around so that the open ends are facing you.

2. Fold the bottom edges of the top flaps only into the middle crease.

3. Turn the paper over and repeat step 2 on the other side.

4. Half unfold one flap so that it sticks up in the air. Push it open and flatten it down.

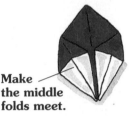

Make the middle folds meet.

Fold this flap across.

Both sides now look like this.

Fold the top layer only.

5. Fold up the other flap and flatten the corner in the same way as in step 4.

6. Turn the paper over once again and repeat steps 4 and 5 on the other side.

7. Fold the left flap over the right. Turn the paper over and repeat on other side.

8. Fold in the sides along the creases already there. Then turn the paper over.

These boxes are ideal as packagings for small gifts.

Bend both ways.

Leave these parts on the table.

Make the fold for step 12 here.

9. Fold in the sides in the same way, on the other side of the paper.

10. Fold down the top at the widest part. Bend it back the other way, too.

11. Fold the top flap only up to the cross where the two creases meet.

For a stronger box cut some thin cardboard to the same size as its bottom and fit it inside.

12. Fold up again, where the plain side meets the decorated side of the paper.

13. Turn the left flap to the right and then repeat steps 11 and 12 on this side.

Pinch around the bottom edges of the box to make the base firmer.

14. Turn the paper over. Repeat steps 11-13 so your paper looks like the picture above.

Push up

15. Pick up the box. Put your fingers inside to open it. It may help to push up the bottom.

Interlocking gift boxes

These boxes make stylish packagings for gifts. You could decorate them with attractive letters traced from the templates on page 93. The instructions here will show you how to make a box about 10cm (4in) across.

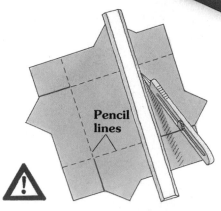

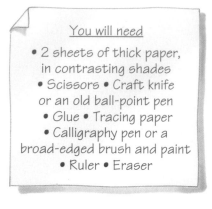

20cm (8in)

20cm (8in)

Join up the marks at the dotted lines with a faint pencil line.

5cm (2in)

1. To make a box measuring 10 x 10cm (4 x 4in), start by drawing a 20 x 20cm (8 x 8in) square on both pieces of paper. Measure and mark points lightly in pencil every 5cm (2in) along each side.

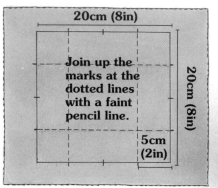

2.5cm (1in)

12.5cm (5in)

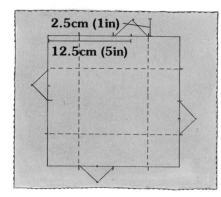

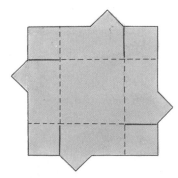

Pencil lines

2. Mark 12.5cm (5in) along each side on both squares. Draw a dot 2.5cm (1in) above each of these marks. Join each dot to the marks on the square either side of it.

3. Using scissors, carefully cut out the two halves of the box along the outlines. Also cut along the red lines indicated in the picture above. Don't cut the dotted lines, though.

4. Gently score along all the dotted lines shown above with a craft knife or an old ball-point pen. Remove all your pencil lines from each box with an eraser.

Decorating with letters

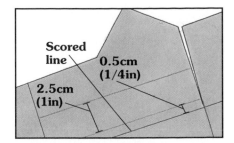

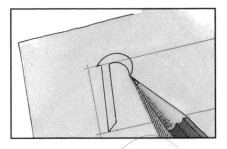

1. Decorate your box before you glue it. Draw two faint pencil lines 0.5cm (¼in) and 2.5cm (1in) from the scored lines, to use as guidelines.

2. Trace over the guidelines onto a piece of tracing paper. Use them to help you trace from the letters shown on page 93.

3. Transfer the lettering to the side or top of the lid. Use either a pen or a broad-edged brush and paint to fill in the letters.

To make a box with wavy edges, open a pair of compasses to 2.5cm (1in) and draw a semicircle at the 12.5cm (5in) mark (see step 2).

You could trace the letters so they make a message for the person who will receive your box.

Finishing off

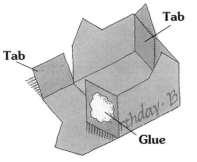

1. Fold up the edges and bend each tab at right angles to the fold. Glue the tabs inside.

2. Finally, interlock the two halves, making sure that all the triangles are on the inside of the box.

Different-sized boxes

To make a different-sized box, draw a square with sides twice as long as you want them to be when the box is complete. To find out the distance between the marks in step 1, divide the length of the side by four. The height of the points in step 2 is half the distance between these marks.

Cancan pigs card

This card is lots of fun to make – and even more fun to receive. You could adapt the basic idea to show all sorts of dancers.

Making the card

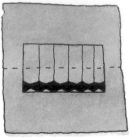
You will need
• Two pieces of thin pink cardboard 15 x 16cm (6 x 6½in) • Felt-tips
• Scissors • Paper doily • Glue
• Glitter, sequins, feathers and stars for extra decorations

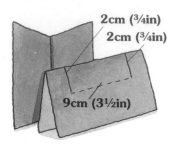

2cm (¾in)
2cm (¾in)
9cm (3½in)

Fold line

1. Fold two pieces of pink card along their longest edges. On one card draw and cut the lines shown above.

2. Crease the fold line but do not push the box through. Mark off the box into six equal strips for legs.

3. Cut along the lines. Open the card and push the box shape through, so it looks like the picture above.

4. Smooth the card out flat. Draw and shade a foot at the end of each leg, using a black felt-tip.

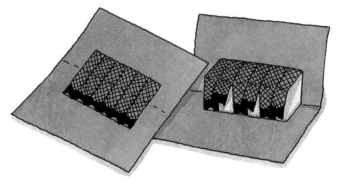

5. Cover the legs with a pattern of criss-cross lines using a very fine black felt-tip pen.

6. Snip across the base of legs 2, 4, and 6 so that they kick. Trim the ends of the feet.

7. Turn the card over. Using felt-tips, decorate the back of each leg with criss-cross lines.

8. Turn the card over again and glue it to the second card. Bend the legs to make them kick.

9. Cut up a paper doily for petticoats. Stick them around the legs. Then draw the pigs' heads and arms, emerging from their lifted dresses.

10. Add feather headdresses to the pigs. You could cut pieces from a feather duster to make them.

11. Smear a little glue here and there on the card, then sprinkle glitter, stars or sequins onto it.

Another idea
You might prefer to draw different sorts of dancers. You could give them legs that don't match.

MASKS, HATS AND BEADS

Using simple sheets of paper or cardboard you can make decorative hats, beautiful masks and paper beads (which you can turn into bangles, necklaces and earrings).

For many of these projects you'll need to trace the templates that appear on pages 94-95. There are tips on successful tracing and scoring on pages 86 and 87.

Take extra care whenever you see a red warning triangle.

Easy masks

All these masks are easy to make. They are ideal for wearing at theme parties, where you need to dress up as a certain type of character.

Wolf mask

Trim the plate to shape the mask.

1. Take a paper plate and use scissors to cut holes for your eyes and a space for your nose.

2. Next, cut a section from a small yogurt carton, as shown in the picture above.

3. Tape the yogurt carton onto the plate, so that the cut in the carton points down.

4. Add ears and a nose cut from the stiff paper. Trim away any sharp edges.

Cut along these lines.

The elastic will hold the mask on your face.

You could paint the mask if you like.

Glue the teeth around the cut you made in the carton.

5. Fold some paper as shown above, and cut along the lines to make teeth. Then glue the teeth around the cut section of the yogurt carton.

6. Poke holes at the sides of the plate and tie some elastic* through them.

Little Piggy

Follow instructions 1-4 for the wolf mask, but cut down the yogurt carton to make the snout shorter. Make shorter ears and don't add teeth. Paint the mask pink. You could add blobs of muddy brown paint to make Piggy look dirty.

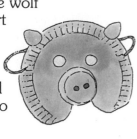

Bear

Follow instructions 1-4 for the wolf mask. Then add round ears and glue on a button nose. Draw on a mouth and dot some whiskers around the nose and mouth. Finally, paint the face light brown and the ears and nose dark brown.

* The best elastic to use is shirring elastic (available from dressmakers' stores). However, a long elastic band that you've cut to form a long strand will do.

Eye masks

This mask has had glue put around the eye holes and glitter sprinkled onto the glue.

This one has feathers stuck over it.

The elastic should be about 38cm (15in) long.

1. Trace the mask template on page 94. Transfer it onto some thin cardboard, then cut it out carefully.

2. Make small slits in the mask as shown on the template then thread elastic through them and knot the ends.

3. You can decorate the masks in any way that you like. You might wish to copy the decorations shown above.

Bug-eyed beast

You could decorate the ends of the cups so that your bug eyes look really strange.

Make yourself into a bug-eyed beast by sticking paper cups onto your basic mask shape. Cut eye holes in the bottoms of the cups before you glue them in place.

You could make antennae for your beast mask by taping pipe cleaners onto the backs of the masks. Bend the ends over and crunch silver paper around the pipe cleaners in balls.

Animal masks

Paint the masks to look like animals. To make whiskers, glue paper drinking straws on either side. Stick on paper ears.

For a cat mask, include ears and cat-like markings.

For a rabbit mask, include long ears. Decorate most of the mask grey-brown.

Paper jewels

You can make necklaces and earrings, as well as brooches and bracelets, out of bits of paper, drinking straw and string. For a really eye-catching effect, use brightly decorated paper or gold or silver paper.

Making the necklace

1. Cut strips of patterned paper to the length of a straw and about 8cm (3in) wide. Cover the paper strips with glue on the plain side.

2. Lay a straw on one long edge and roll the paper. Leave it to dry. Then wrap several more pieces of paper around it, one by one.

3. Cut the straw into small pieces. If the ends flatten, squeeze them into round shapes again.

Try cutting small squares of wrapping paper to thread between the beads.

If you have no wrapping paper, decorate some white paper yourself, or use pages from an old magazine.

Quick brooches

1. Cut out pictures you like, or draw your own. Stick them to pieces of cereal box.

2. Attach a safety pin at the back using tape to make a brooch.

4. Thread the beads with fine wool or elastic, using a needle to pull the yarn through. When the necklace is long enough to slip over your head, tie the yarn in a knot.

Matching earrings

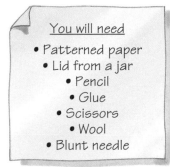
You can make earrings to match your beads with the help of these simple instructions.

1. Draw around a small jar lid to make a circle. Then cut the circle out.

2. Fold the circle in half. Cut it along the fold line to make two halves.

3. Put a strip of glue halfway along the straight edge of each half circle.

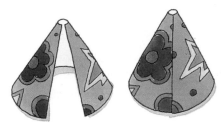

4. Bend around and overlap the edges to make a cone. Stick it down firmly. Snip the top off the cone.

Loop some yarn through the cone using a blunt needle to help you thread it through.

Glue the ends inside the cone. Then hang the loop over your ear.

Quick bracelets

1. Cut out two strips of different shades of paper. One should fit around your wrist, the other one should be much longer.

2. Wrap the long piece around the shorter piece to give a striped effect. Join the ends with adhesive tape to make a circle. Glue down the ends and trim them.

Make some paper beads out of drinking straws covered with paper (see steps 1 and 2 of "Making the necklace" on the opposite page). Then thread a short piece of yarn or string through them to make a bracelet.

Hovering bee mask

For this eye-catching mask, first trace the basic mask template on page 94 onto thin cardboard and then cut it out. The special equipment you will need for this project is florists' wire and about 1m (3ft) of fine elastic.*

Making the mask

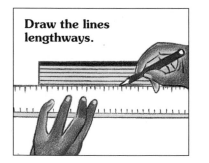

1. Trace the basic mask shape and cut it out. Attach elastic and then cut out the eyeholes.

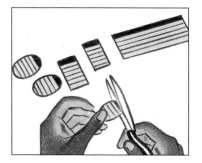

2. Cut out flowers and leaves from the wrapping paper. Glue them onto the mask to cover it, as shown below.

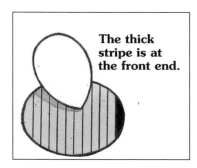

3. Cut the wires to lengths of 10-15cm (4-6in). Bend the ends of each and tape them to the back of the mask.

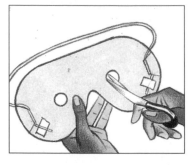

Draw the lines lengthways.

4. For the bees, draw black lines across the yellow paper with a ruler and a felt-tip pen. Do a really thick line at the top.

5. Cut the paper into twelve 2cm (½in) pieces. Now round off the corners of each piece to make fat bee shapes.

The thick stripe is at the front end.

6. Cut out 12 teardrop shapes from white paper. Glue one onto each bee, slanting them slightly away from the front.

7. Turn over the mask so that it is right side down. Slip a bee face down behind the tip of each wire and tape it on.

Arranging the flowers

Starting at the edge of the mask, glue the flowers on. Let them stick out over the edge of the mask.

Don't worry if some of the flowers cover the eyeholes. You can trim them back when the glue is dry.

* Florist's wire is available at your local florists'. You can buy fine quality elastic, called shirring elastic, from sewing stores.

The bees on this mask will move and hover as you walk.

Lightly bend the wires.

Another idea

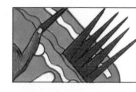

Cut out wavy strips of green and silver paper and stick them to the basic mask shape.

Make pointed reeds from strips of cardboard. Glue them to the top of the mask.

Tape wires on (as in step 3 on the previous page) and put fish shapes on their tops.

Octopus and clown masks

These jolly masks will cover your whole head. They're simple to make but you'll need to use some vinyl wallpaper to make them. You may need to buy a roll from a shop. Alternatively, see if there is any unwanted wallpaper at home that you could use.

You will need
(for the octopus mask)
• Vinyl wallpaper 100cm (40in) long
• Vinyl wallpaper 75cm (30in) long
• Thick paint, orange and green • Pencil
• Sponge • Stapler • Paper clips • Scissors

Making the octopus mask

Decorate the plain side if the wallpaper is patterned.

Copy the head shape from the picture below.

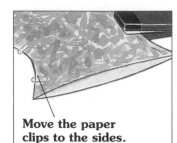

Move the paper clips to the sides.

1. Dab the wallpaper with a sponge dipped in green paint. Let it dry, then wipe with a damp sponge to get a pale, watery look.

2. Fold the short edges of the larger piece of paper. Use paper clips to hold the ends together. Draw a large octopus head.

3. Carefully cut out the shape, moving the paper clips to the edges. Now staple the edges, leaving the bottom open.

4. Put the mask on and ask a friend to help you mark places for the eyeholes. Take off the mask and cut out the eyeholes.

Tentacles

1. Fold the smaller piece of wallpaper in half along its length. Then repeat this two more times, so that you make a long shape.

2. Open out the paper and cut along the folds to make eight strips.

3. Finally, take each strip and trim one end into a slightly rounded point.

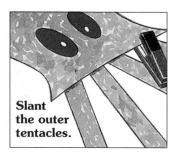

Slant the outer tentacles.

5. Paint large orange eyes around the eyeholes. Put the tentacles a little way inside the mask, four at the front and four at the back. Then staple them to the mask.

For maximum effect, you could make bubbling noises when you wear this mask, to give the impression that you are underwater.

Clown mask

1. To begin, cut out the basic head shape by copying the shape of the octopus head shown on the opposite page.

2. Cut long crêpe paper strips 6cm (2½in) wide. Pleat and staple them around the curved edge of one of the head shapes.

3. Place the other head shape on top of the frilled half and staple the curved edges together. Keep the plain side facing up.

4. Cut eyeholes (see step 4 on the opposite page) and then paint on a mouth. Add a nose and eyebrows and paint the eyes.

To make your mask even brighter than this one you could use glitter to outline the eyes, mouth and nose.

5. Cut a piece of stiff cardboard about 12 x 7cm (5 x 3in) and glue it to the inside bottom edge of the mask.

6. Make a huge bow out of crêpe paper. Glue it onto the mask, below the level of the clown's chin.

Paper beads and bangles

These beads are made by tightly wrapping little strips of paper around themselves. Use the large photograph to inspire you for the style of decoration, or copy the ones that you like the most. Then simply thread them onto lengths of yarn, string or strips of leather to make necklaces or bangles.

Making tapered beads

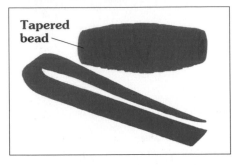

1. Cut a paper strip about 3 x 40cm (1 x 16in). From the middle of its length, cut both sides of the strip so that it forms a point at one end.

2. Coat a knitting needle with a thin layer of petroleum jelly. Then brush a thin layer of wallpaper paste over the back of the strip of paper.

3. Roll the strip around the knitting needle a few times to form a hole, then slip it off and roll by hand. Make all the beads in this way.

Making small, straight beads

Cut straight strips of paper 1.5 x 40cm (½ x 16in). Then paste them and roll them up around a knitting needle, as you would for the tapered beads.

The straight beads on this necklace and the bangle next to it have been decorated using fine felt-tips in a style based on a South American design.

Threading the beads

Before you thread your beads decide how you are going to arrange them. Thread them so you create a bangle or necklace with a pleasing arrangement, not one that is simply a jumble of beads.

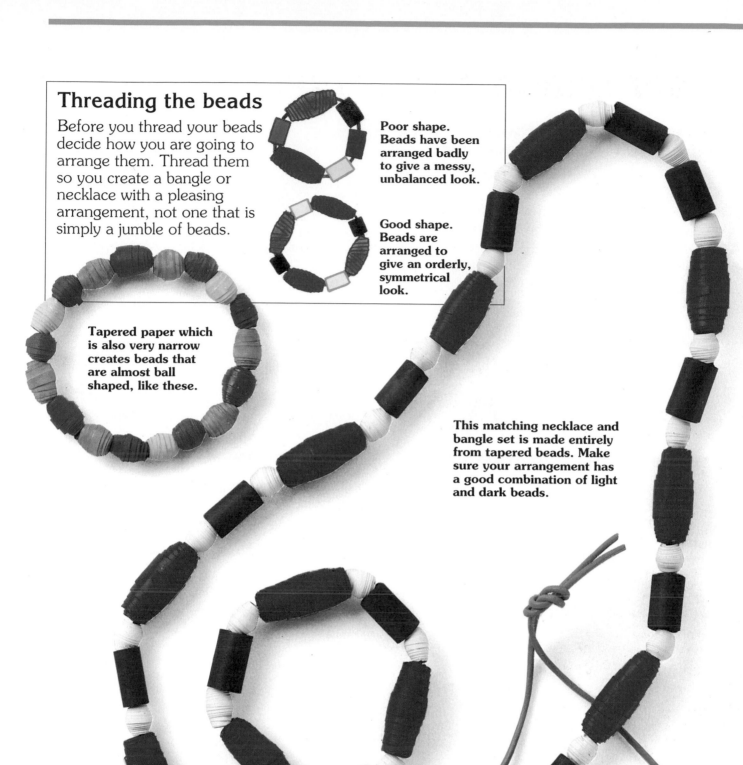

Poor shape. Beads have been arranged badly to give a messy, unbalanced look.

Good shape. Beads are arranged to give an orderly, symmetrical look.

Tapered paper which is also very narrow creates beads that are almost ball shaped, like these.

This matching necklace and bangle set is made entirely from tapered beads. Make sure your arrangement has a good combination of light and dark beads.

By filling an elastic thread with beads, you can create a necklace or bangle with a hidden knot, like this one. Stretch the elastic slightly before you knot it.

A few simple beads threaded around a short leather strip makes an attractive choker-style necklace.

Extra-large beads are ideal for adding detailed decorations.

Movie star masks

These masks are ideal to make if you want to pretend that you are a character in a movie. You will have to make a simple basic mask to go beneath each of the two masks shown here. The template for the basic mask is on page 94.

Detective mask

1. Trace the template on page 94 onto some thin cardboard. Go over the lines in black (keep the tracing to use later).

2. Cut around the mask shape and snip out the eyeholes. Paint the hatband and the frame of the glasses.

3. Cut out the glasses' lenses from your tracing. Lay them over black plastic and draw the shapes onto the plastic.

4. Cut out the plastic shapes, leaving 1cm (½in) all around. Then snip out the eyeholes and glue the plastic lenses onto the mask.

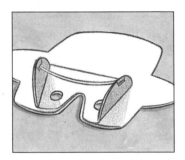

5. Glue the front of the basic mask to the back of the main mask. Attach elastic to the flaps.

Paint some stubble on your face to finish off the disguise.

You could complete your costume by wearing a big raincoat as shown here.

Superstar

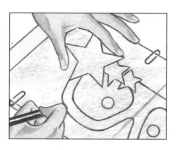

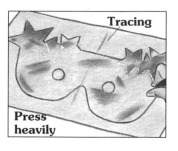

This mask could be part of an extravagant costume. You could pretend to be an outrageous superstar when you wear it.

1. Trace and copy the template on page 95 onto a piece of thin cardboard. Keep the tracing – you will need it later.

2. Carefully cut out the shape. Spread glue over the front of the mask then lay it face down onto a piece of kitchen foil.

3. Turn over the mask and trim the edges and eyeholes. Lay the tracing over the top and pencil over the stars.

Add more glitter to the mask for a really dazzling effect.

Wear flamboyant clothes, such as a feather boa and black silk gloves.

4. Stick on the black plastic lenses and tie a length of elastic to the basic mask. See steps 3-5 on the opposite page to find out how to do this.

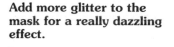

5. Go around all the edges and points of the stars with glue and glitter or a glitter pen.

Headdresses

These headdresses could be the crowning glory of a special costume. Wear them to theme parties, to create a stir when you arrive.

You will need
• Black or dark blue thin cardboard 50 x 50cm (20 x 20in)
• Silver paper • Scissors • Glue
• Adhesive tape • Thin paper strips
• Decorations, such as gold and silver thread, and crêpe paper to make flowers (see page 27)

Curl the ends of thin paper strips and tape them to the top of the hat.

Fairytale princess's hat

1. Take the square of thin cardboard and fold it into a cone. Secure it with some adhesive tape.

2. Trim the bottom edge with scissors to make it straight. Then glue on decorations as shown in the photograph.

Sun hat

You will need
• Thin cardboard 55 x 55cm (22 x 22in)
• Crêpe paper • Tissue paper • Pencil • String
• Scissors • Adhesive tape • Crêpe paper to make flowers (see page 27)

Slits

50cm (20in)

1. Using cardboard, draw and cut out a circle 50cm (20in) across. Cut two slits opposite each other, 8cm (3in) from the middle.

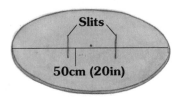

2. Cut a ribbon of crêpe paper about 10cm (4in) wide and 100cm (40in) long. Fold it in half lengthways and thread it through the slits. Make some paper flowers (see page 27) and glue them onto the hat using adhesive tape.

Wrap silver and gold threads around the hat. Hold them on with adhesive tape.

Decorate the bottom of the hat with paper flowers. You could make them by following the instructions on page 27. Don't make the stems though.

Decorate the yellow base of the sun hat by drawing a pattern on it, as shown in the photo. From a distance it will look as if it is made from straw.

Feather headdress

You will need
- Corrugated cardboard 50 x 5cm (20 x 2in)
- Tissue paper
- Drinking straws
- Scissors • Glue
- Adhesive tape
- Paint or felt-tips

1. Paint a pattern onto the corrugated cardboard. When it is dry, attach the two ends using adhesive tape.

2. Cut some feather shapes out of tissue paper. Make them a little shorter than the drinking straws.

4. Glue the feathers onto the straws. Leave about 5cm (2in) of straw pointing out beneath each feather.

5. Make little cuts all along both sides of the feathers, as shown in the picture above.

6. Push the ends of the straws into the holes in the corrugated cardboard. Make sure you have a good variety of different feathers next to each other. For example, put yellow ones next to green ones next to red ones.

Tiger mask

Use the templates on page 95 to trace this fierce tiger. You could use the basic design to make other big cats, such as a panther, leopard or a lion.

You will need
- Stiff orange paper • Thin white cardboard
- Scissors • Glue • Black felt-tip pen
- Ruler • Adhesive tape • Paintbrush
- Black, white, yellow and red paints
- Tracing paper • Pencil • Paper clip

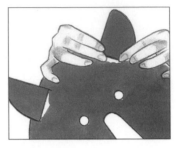

1. Trace and cut out all the shapes copied from the template. Carefully snip out the eyeholes using scissors.

2. Take the ears and turn one over to make a left and right ear. Bend the inner corner of each and glue them down. Let them dry.

3. Paint the pieces, using the main photo as a guide. Outline the features in black. Paint the iris of each eye bright yellow.

4. Glue the ears behind the face, between the marks at the top. Place the ears so the folded sides face each other. Let the glue dry.

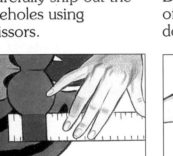

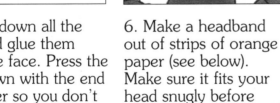

5. Fold down all the tabs and glue them onto the face. Press the tabs down with the end of a ruler so you don't squash the shape.

6. Make a headband out of strips of orange paper (see below). Make sure it fits your head snugly before you tape it.

Copy the markings shown in this photograph.

Cut long, thin pointed whiskers in different lengths from white cardboard. Glue the unpointed ends onto the muzzle.

Securing the mask

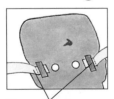

Cut two strips of thick paper. Glue the ends to the back of the mask.

For a harder wearing headband, glue extra tabs here.

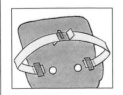

Wrap the strips around your head. Secure the strips with a paper clip, then tape them together.

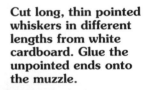

FLYING THINGS

Flying paper toys can come in all sorts of shapes and sizes, ranging from simple paper planes through to flying paper birds, origami models and kites. This section contains instructions to all these projects – and others.

Many of the models will need to be traced from templates on page 96. You can find extra tips to help your tracing techniques on pages 86-87.

To avoid injury, take extra care whenever you see an instruction that has a red warning triangle next to it.

Mini jets

You can make these tiny planes from single pieces of ordinary writing paper. The one on this page can be adjusted so you can control the way it flies.

Making a V-jet

Cut here.

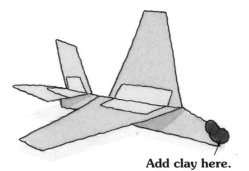

1. Trace the V-jet template from page 96 onto a piece of folded paper. Place the straight bottom edge of the template on the fold.

2. Score along the blue lines and cut along the red line. The bottom blue line changes angle at the slit, so score each side separately.

3. Bend the wings and the tail out to the sides along the score lines. The wings should point up slightly. The tail should make a "V" shape.

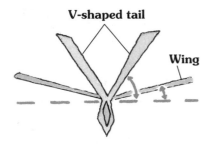
V-shaped tail **Wing**

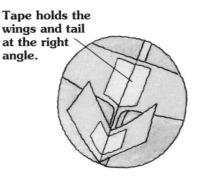
Tape holds the wings and tail at the right angle.

Add clay here.

4. Check that your plane looks like the picture above, from behind. Then use tape to hold the wings and tail at the correct angles.

5. You should position the tape so that the wings are pointing up slightly. Tape the tail so it points up more steeply than the wings.

6. Put a little clay inside the nose. Then test fly the plane. If it flies up, then stops and falls, add more clay. If it dives, take some clay away.

Steering your V-jet

To make the V-jet turn, alter the shapes of the tail tips. To do this curl the tip between your finger and thumb, as shown below.

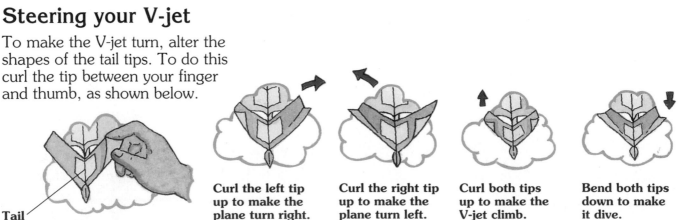

Tail

Curl the left tip up to make the plane turn right.

Curl the right tip up to make the plane turn left.

Curl both tips up to make the V-jet climb.

Bend both tips down to make it dive.

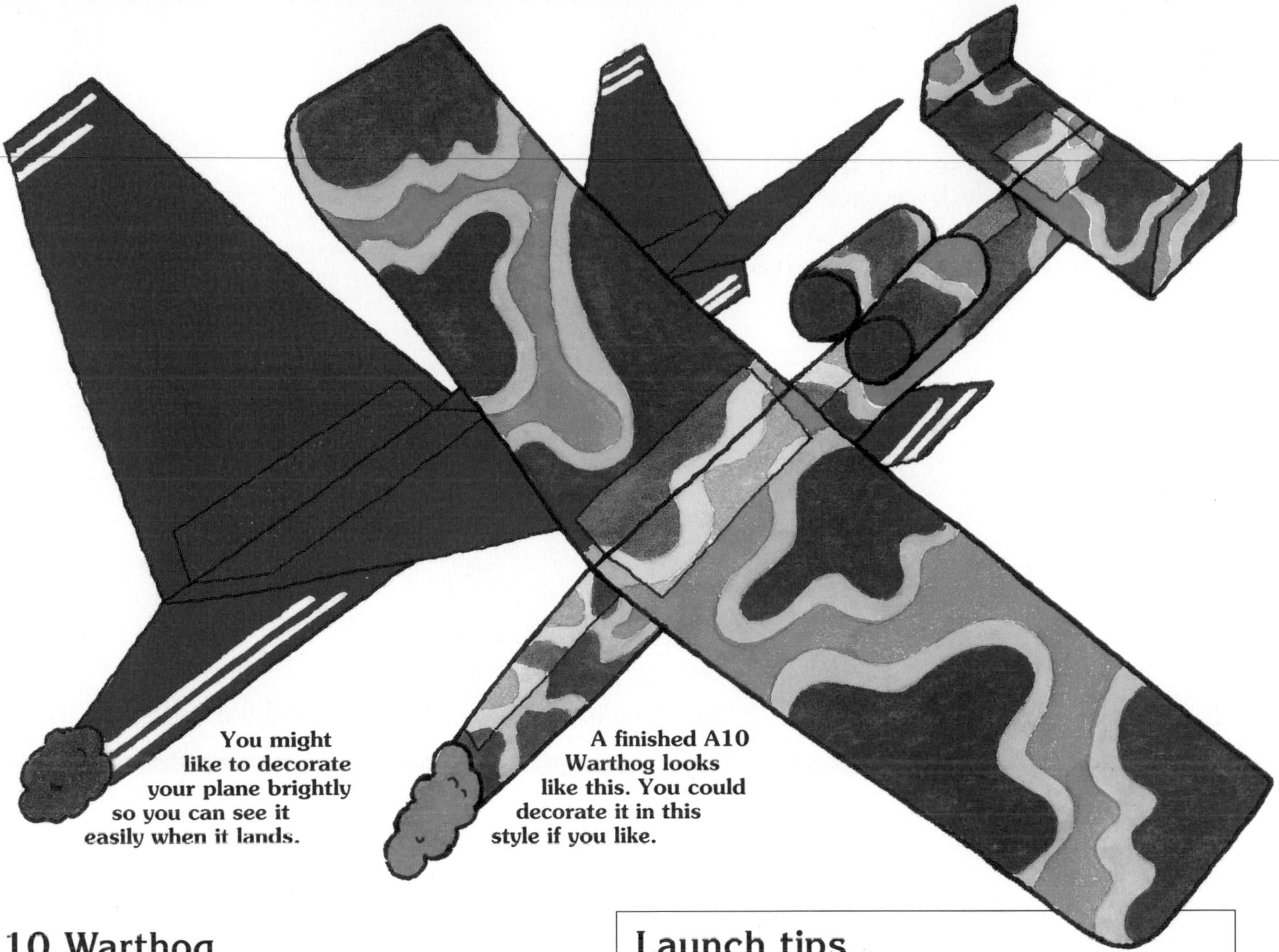

You might like to decorate your plane brightly so you can see it easily when it lands.

A finished A10 Warthog looks like this. You could decorate it in this style if you like.

A10 Warthog

This plane is based on an old US Air Force jet, with engines behind the wings. Use the template on page 96 to trace the shape.

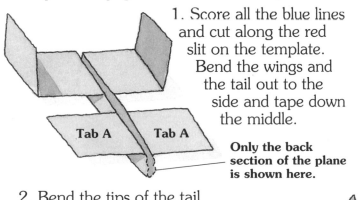

1. Score all the blue lines and cut along the red slit on the template. Bend the wings and the tail out to the side and tape down the middle.

Tab A   **Tab A**

Only the back section of the plane is shown here.

2. Bend the tips of the tail along the score lines so they stick up in the air as shown above.

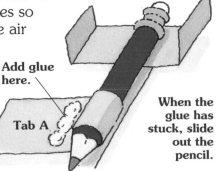

Add glue here.

Only the back section of the plane is shown here.

Tab A

When the glue has stuck, slide out the pencil.

3. Tabs A are for the engines. Roll them around a pencil and tape them down in the middle.

Launch tips

These tips should help you to get the most out of your mini jets. If they don't fly well, try changing their balance by adjusting the shape of the wings slightly.

High launches

The higher you stand when you launch your planes, the further they will fly. You might like to stand on a chair and see how far they will glide when you launch them from up there.

Gentle launches

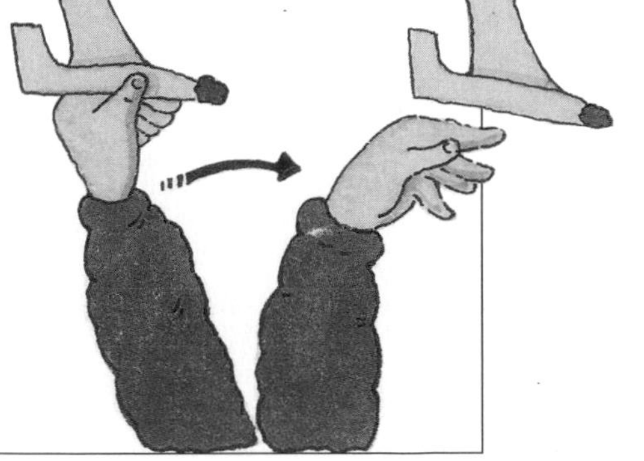

Light planes like these fly best if you don't throw them hard. To launch one, hold it underneath the wings. Then move your whole arm forward and simply let go. It should soar off.

Camber jet

Like all modern jets, this plane has curved wings, called cambered wings. These help to lift it up into the air, so it flies more effortlessly than a plane with straight wings.

Making the camber jet

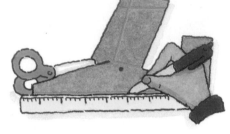

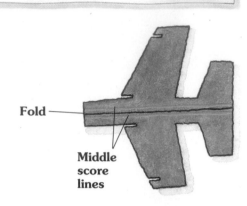

Fold

Middle score lines

1. Fold the stiff paper in half along its longest sides. Then trace the template on page 96 onto the paper.

2. Cut along the red lines. Score the blue ones firmly with an old ball-point pen so that it creases both sides.

3. This plane has a flat bottom so you need to unfold the paper and flatten the fold down its middle.

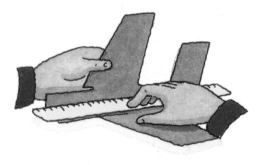

Tabs A

Wing tip

4. Fold along one of the middle score lines. Make the fold against a ruler to create a really neat, accurate crease.

5. Turn the paper around. Fold along the other score line so sides of the plane stand up in the air.

6. Bend the wings and the tail along the score lines, shown in blue, so that they stick out to the side.

7. Fold along the score line of each of the tabs marked "A" (see picture A on the right). Then put some glue on the undersides of these tabs, as shown in picture B. Next, stick them to the inside of the body of the plane, called the fuselage (see picture C).

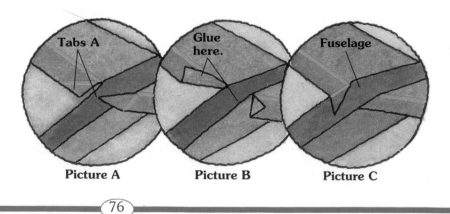

Tabs A

Glue here.

Fuselage

Picture A **Picture B** **Picture C**

Making the cambered wings

Fold the tip of each wing down along
the score line. Bend back the triangular
tabs marked "B", as shown in picture
A on the right. Next, glue each tab,
as directed in picture B. Then bend
along the lines parallel to the edges
of the wings and tape the tabs
underneath (see picture C).
The wings should curve.

Tab B

Glue
here.

Bend
here.

Picture A **Picture B** **Picture C**

Checking the balance

Look under the wings of your plane for
the dots you traced from the template.
These mark the balance point of the
plane. Place the wings on the tips
of two pencils, alongside the dots.

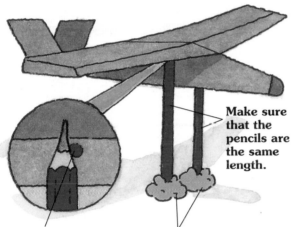

**Make sure
that the
pencils are
the same
length.**

**Dot traced from
the template.**

**Hold the pencils
upright in some clay.**

If you find that the plane falls back,
you should add some clay to the nose.
If it falls forward you should take some
away. When the plane balances, the
wings will be at the correct angle for
the jet to fly successfully.

How a wing lifts

When a wing goes forward, some air goes
over the top of it and some goes below it. If
the wing is curved, the air on top has further
to go than the air below. So it stretches to
catch up with the bottom air. This makes it
thinner, and sucks the wing up.

**Thinner air pulls
the wing up.**

Wing

**Normal
air**

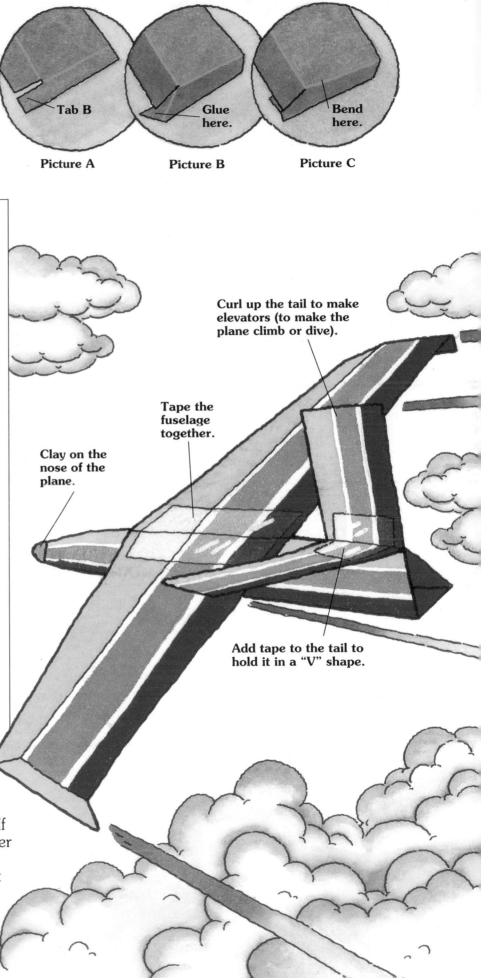

**Curl up the tail to make
elevators (to make the
plane climb or dive).**

**Tape the
fuselage
together.**

**Clay on the
nose of the
plane.**

**Add tape to the tail to
hold it in a "V" shape.**

Paper birds

These models look like birds but they fly just like paper planes. The instructions show you how to make the seagull, but by modifying the basic shape and markings slightly you can make the swallow as well.

Making the seagull

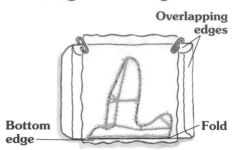

Overlapping edges

Bottom edge — Fold

You could use a ball-point pen to score your lines.

1. Fold the paper in half along its longest sides. Copy the template (see page 96) onto the paper, making sure that you match the bottom edge of your tracing to the folded edge.

2. Cut out the shape, cutting along the red lines. Score all the blue lines well (using a ruler to keep your scored lines straight). Make sure there is a crease on both sides of the folded shape.

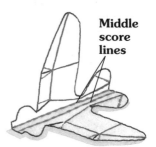

Middle score lines

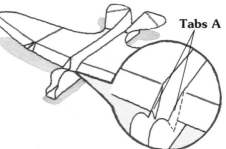

Tabs A

3. Fold the sides up along the middle score lines, to make a flat bottom.

4. Bend the wings and tail out to the side. Then glue tabs A inside the body.

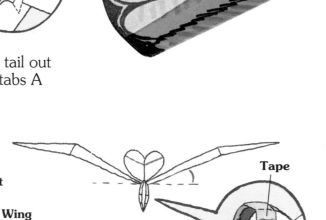

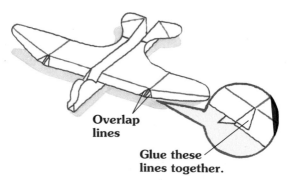

Overlap lines

Glue these lines together.

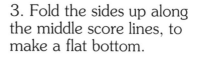

Tail tips

Tape — Slit

— Wing

Tape

Clay

5. Find the two overlap lines on either side of the slit, in the middle of the wing. Put glue on one and slide the other over until the lines meet. Hold them together until they are stuck.

6. Bend the tips of the tail up. Then tape over the slit where the tails and wings join to make the tail stick up slightly. This will help the tail to control the flight of the bird.

7. Check to see that the wings are even and point up slightly. Then test fly your model to see if you need to put clay in the beak. Finally, tape over the head.

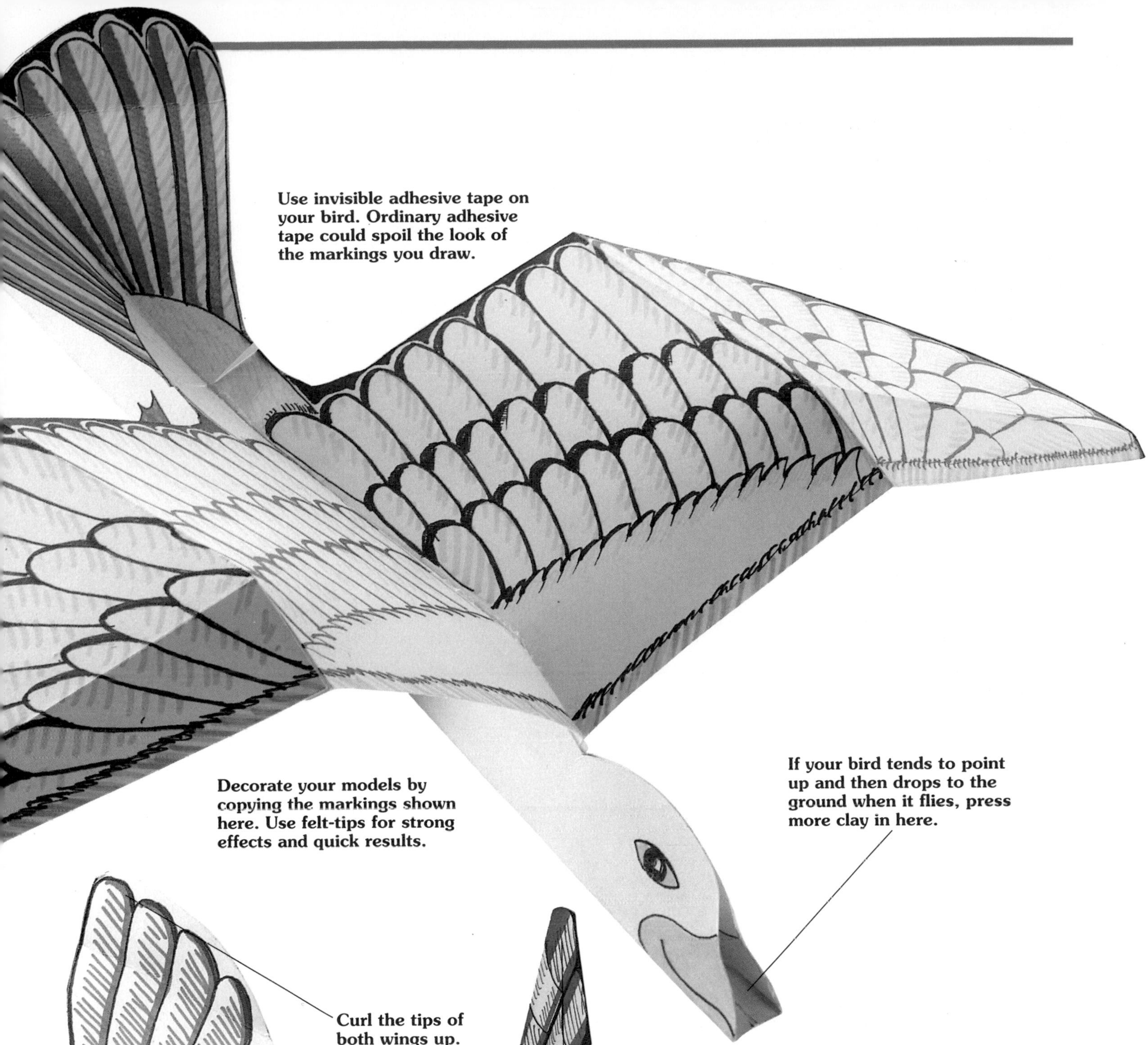

Use invisible adhesive tape on your bird. Ordinary adhesive tape could spoil the look of the markings you draw.

Decorate your models by copying the markings shown here. Use felt-tips for strong effects and quick results.

If your bird tends to point up and then drops to the ground when it flies, press more clay in here.

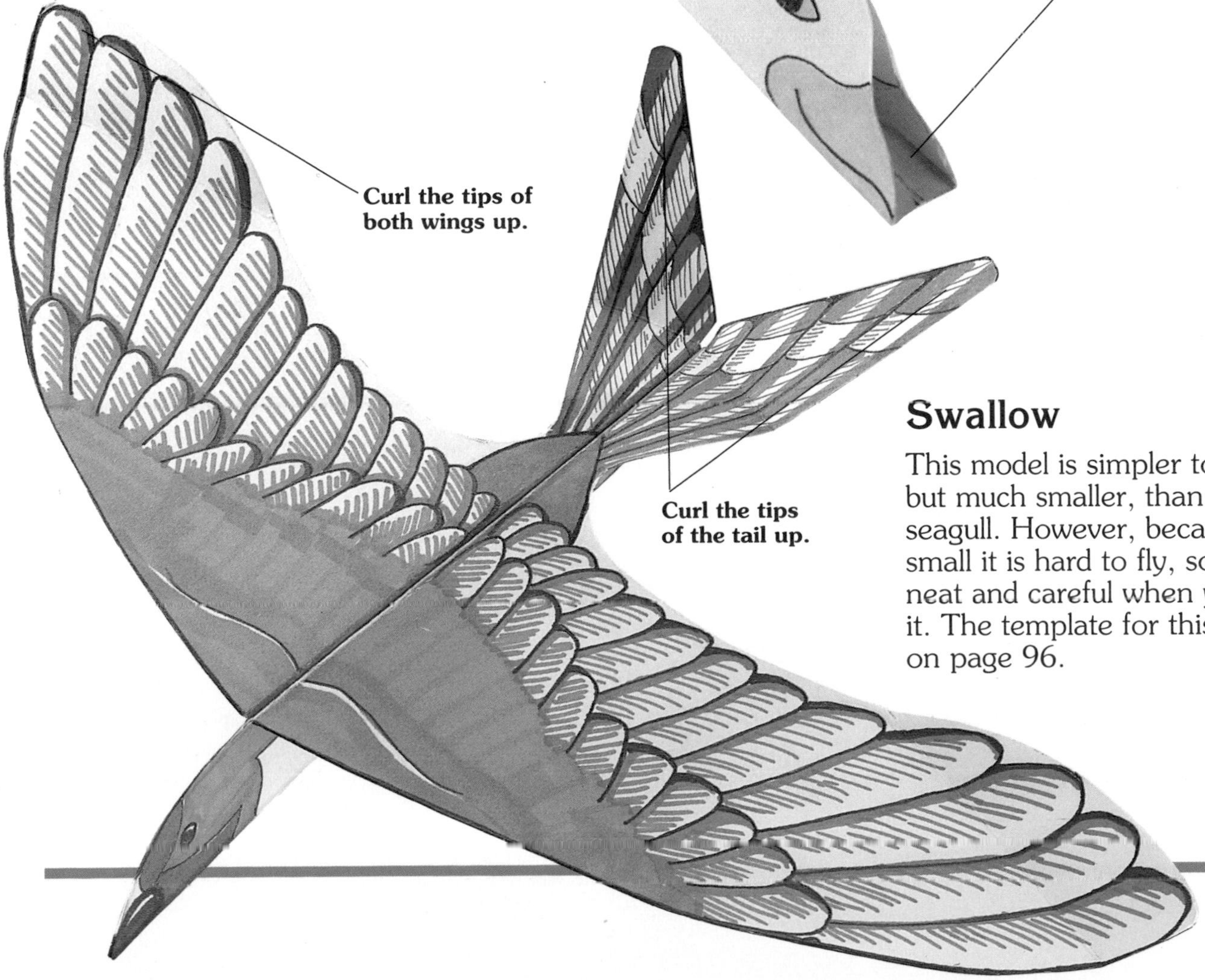

Curl the tips of both wings up.

Curl the tips of the tail up.

Swallow

This model is simpler to make, but much smaller, than the seagull. However, because it is small it is hard to fly, so be very neat and careful when you make it. The template for this model is on page 96.

Flying origami toys

These unusual flying toys are easy to make. The one on this page flutters like a butterfly when you launch it. The one opposite skims the air like a futuristic space ship.*

Making a flutter butterfly

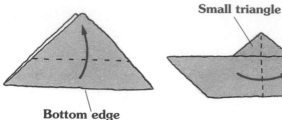

Small triangle

Fold the top layer here.

Bottom edge

1. Turn the paper so one corner is pointing to you, plain side up. Then fold the bottom corner to the top.

2. Fold up the bottom edge, as shown above, so that you leave a small triangle showing at the top.

3. Carefully fold the paper in half from side to side. Make sure that all the edges meet one another neatly.

4. Fold back the top layer along the dotted line marked in the picture above. Fold the top layer only.

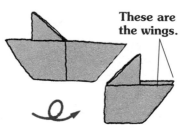

These are the wings.

5. Turn the paper over and fold the other side in exactly the same way.

Flying the butterfly

Make the wings stick out to the sides. Then hold the butterfly's body, beneath the wings, and launch it by throwing it forward gently.

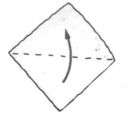

Making a splatter effect design

Make sure you have some newspaper underneath.

1. Fold the square in half diagonally. Then unfold it.

2. Splash some paint on one half of the paper only.

3. Fold it in half and press down hard.

4. Unfold the paper and leave it to dry.

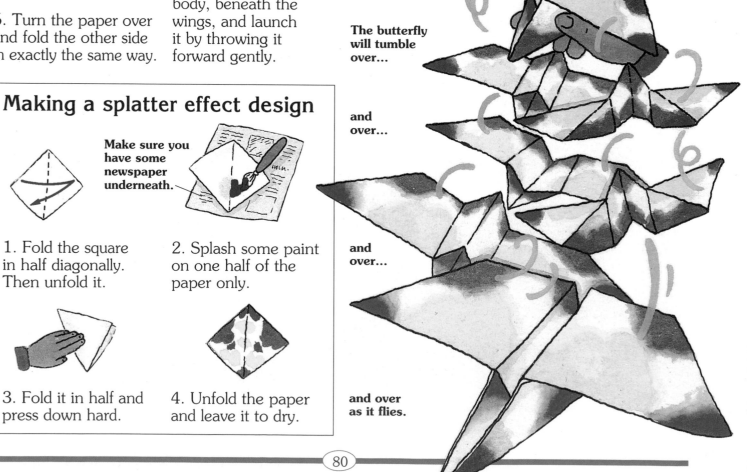

The butterfly will tumble over...

and over...

and over...

and over as it flies.

* **For tips on origami techniques, plus explanations of the symbols used on these pages, see page 87.**

Space spinner

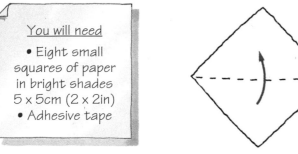
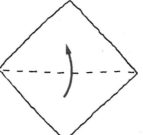

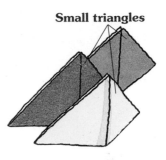

For a really bright effect when you make a space spinner, use fluorescent or shiny paper. Your creation will shimmer as it flies.

1. Take a single square of paper, plain side up, with one corner pointing to you. Fold the bottom corner to the top corner.

2. Fold the bottom right corner up to the top corners so that you make a small triangular flap across the paper.

3. Fold all the other squares in exactly the same way, so that all the pieces look identical, as shown in the picture above.

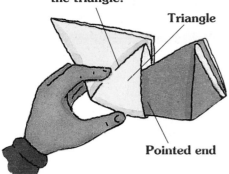

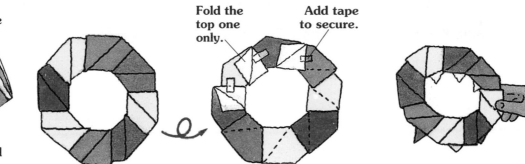

4. Slot the pointed end of each piece of paper inside the small triangular flap of the next one.

5. Keep joining the paper pieces until you have made a complete circle. Then turn the space spinner over.

6. Fold back the top flaps on all the sections so they stick up. Tape the pieces together.

7. To launch your space spinner, throw it flat, like a frisbee. It should spin through the air.

Draw on windows with passengers looking out.

Square-o-plane

All you need to build this simple paper plane is a large piece of paper and a paper clip, plus a pen and a ruler to draw with.

You will need
- Writing paper 21 x 15cm (8 x 6in)
- Ball-point pen • Pencil
- Ruler • Paper clip

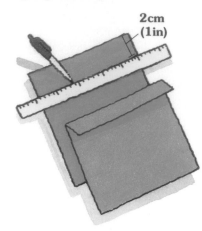

2cm (1in)

1. Score a line 2cm (1in) from the top of one short edge. Then fold along the line that you have made.

Make the last score line here.

2. Score another line at the edge of the last fold and fold over again. Then repeat this once more.

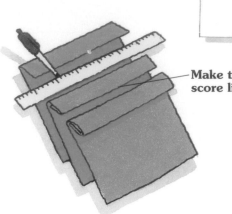

Middle.

3. Turn the paper over so that the folded edge is facing down. Mark the middle of each short edge.

4. Score a line down the middle. Fold along it, then unfold it, so that the sides tilt up slightly.

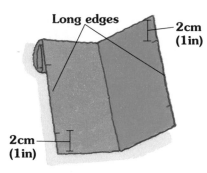

Long edges   **2cm (1in)**

2cm (1in)

5. Make a pencil dot on the long edges, 2cm (1in) from each corner as shown.

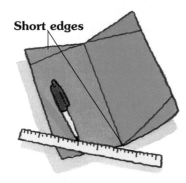

Short edges

6. Score a line from each pencil dot to the middle of the short edge.

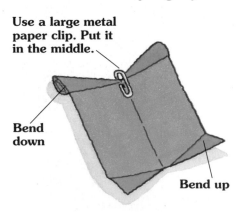

Use a large metal paper clip. Put it in the middle.

Bend down

Bend up

7. Bend the front corners down slightly and the back corners up. Add a paper clip to the front edge.

Checking the shape

Before you launch your plane, check that it looks like the pictures below from the side and from the front.

Side view

The front edge needs to be heavier than the back. The back corners should tilt up. They help to stop the plane from rocking.

Front view

The wings tilt slightly up at the same angle. This helps the plane glide steadily, without suddenly dropping to the ground.

An abstract pattern is very striking on a square-o-plane.

This decoration is based on the shape of a bat in flight.

Use bold felt-tips for stunning decorations.

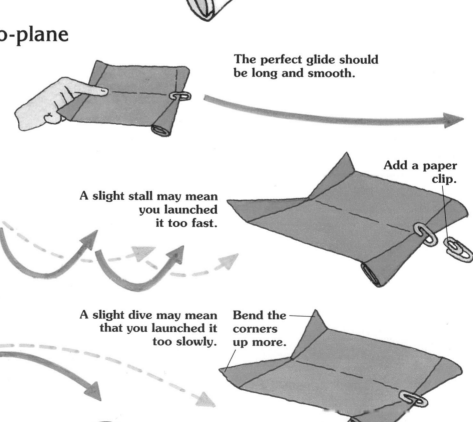

Decorating the planes

You can decorate square-o-planes in all sorts of ways. For instance, you could draw animals on them, or scary faces, or bright patterns. Use felt-tips in bold, contrasting tones for strong effects.

Launching your square-o-plane

Hold the plane at the back with one finger on top. Launch it with a gentle push. Don't throw it, just let go. If it doesn't glide very well, try changing the balance as described below.

The perfect glide should be long and smooth.

Stall

A stall is when the tail drops down because the nose is not heavy enough. Add another paper clip or flatten out the back corners.

A slight stall may mean you launched it too fast.

Add a paper clip.

Dive

A dive is when the nose drops down because it is too heavy. Bend the back corners up, or take away a paper clip.

A slight dive may mean that you launched it too slowly.

Bend the corners up more.

Paperfold kite

You can use almost any type of thin paper to make this kite. You could use plain paper to make a conventional looking kite. By using silver wrapping paper you could make an eye-catching, shimmering version. Because it is made of paper, this kite will fly best in a gentle wind.

Making the kite

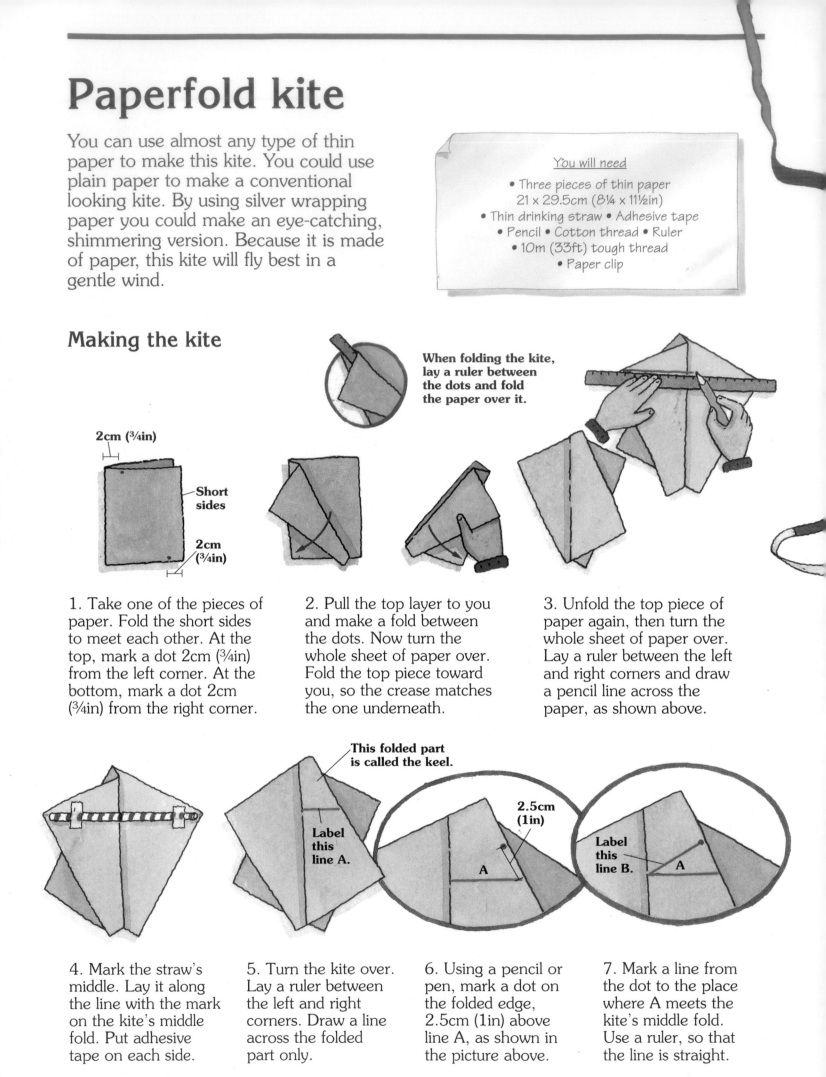

When folding the kite, lay a ruler between the dots and fold the paper over it.

2cm (¾in)

Short sides

2cm (¾in)

1. Take one of the pieces of paper. Fold the short sides to meet each other. At the top, mark a dot 2cm (¾in) from the left corner. At the bottom, mark a dot 2cm (¾in) from the right corner.

2. Pull the top layer to you and make a fold between the dots. Now turn the whole sheet of paper over. Fold the top piece toward you, so the crease matches the one underneath.

3. Unfold the top piece of paper again, then turn the whole sheet of paper over. Lay a ruler between the left and right corners and draw a pencil line across the paper, as shown above.

This folded part is called the keel.

Label this line A.

2.5cm (1in)

A

Label this line B.

A

4. Mark the straw's middle. Lay it along the line with the mark on the kite's middle fold. Put adhesive tape on each side.

5. Turn the kite over. Lay a ruler between the left and right corners. Draw a line across the folded part only.

6. Using a pencil or pen, mark a dot on the folded edge, 2.5cm (1in) above line A, as shown in the picture above.

7. Mark a line from the dot to the place where A meets the kite's middle fold. Use a ruler, so that the line is straight.

Making the reel and kite line

To make a reel, fold another piece of paper in half four times, then fold it in half along its length. Tie a 10m (33ft) length of thread around the reel. Wind it up.

Tie the other end of the thread securely to a paper clip. Push the paper clip firmly onto the kite at line A.

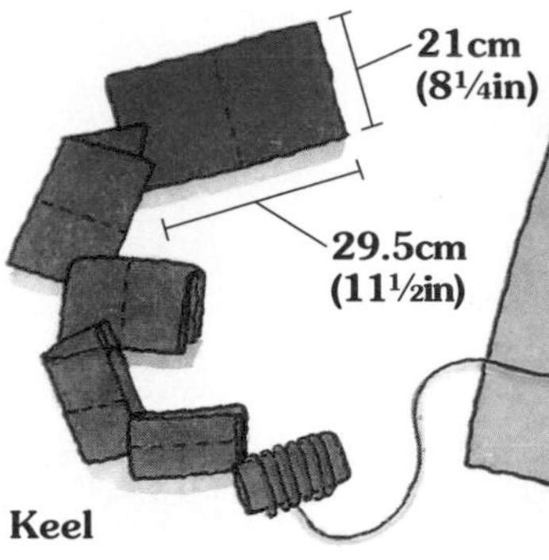

21cm (8¼in)

29.5cm (11½in)

Keel

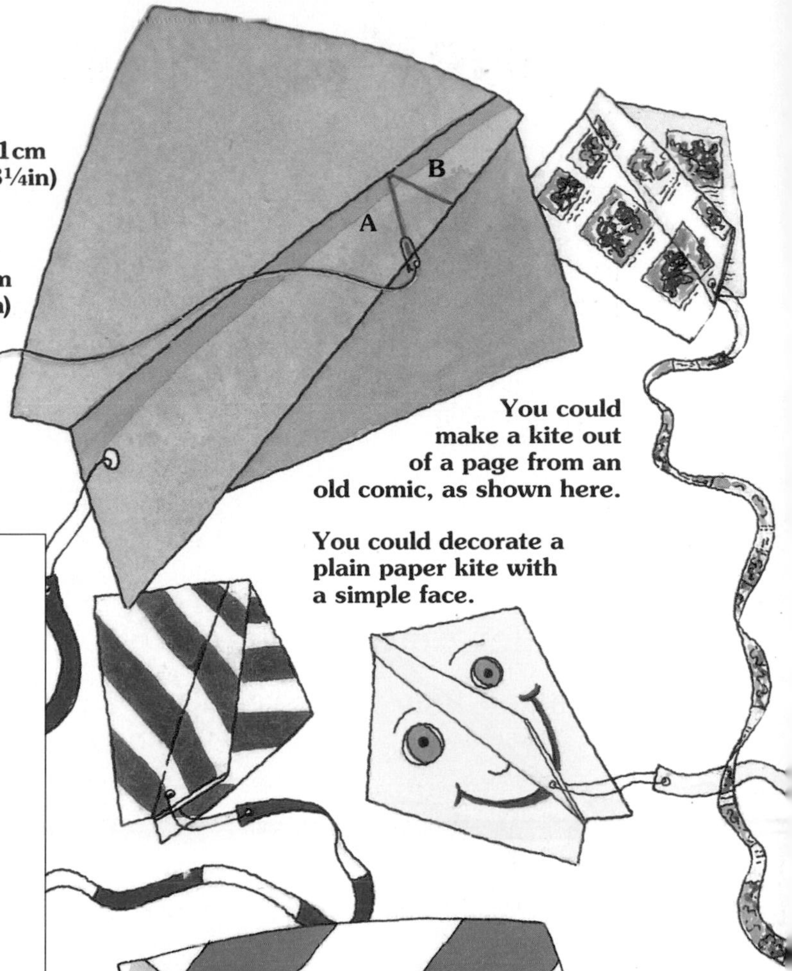

A

B

You could make a kite out of a page from an old comic, as shown here.

You could decorate a plain paper kite with a simple face.

Making the tail

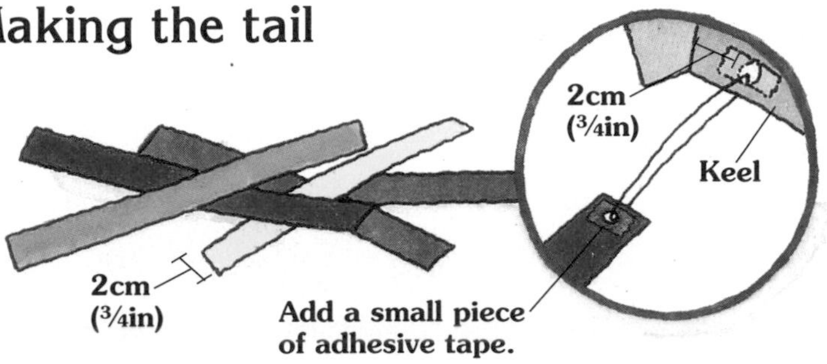

2cm (¾in)

Keel

2cm (¾in)

Add a small piece of adhesive tape.

Cut the last piece of paper into long strips 2cm (¾in) wide. Decorate them and glue them together to make an 80cm (31½in) tail. Make a hole in one end with a pencil.

Make a hole near the bottom of the keel, 2cm (¾in) out from the kite's middle fold. Tie the tail on with a 30cm (12in) piece of thread. Add adhesive tape as shown above.

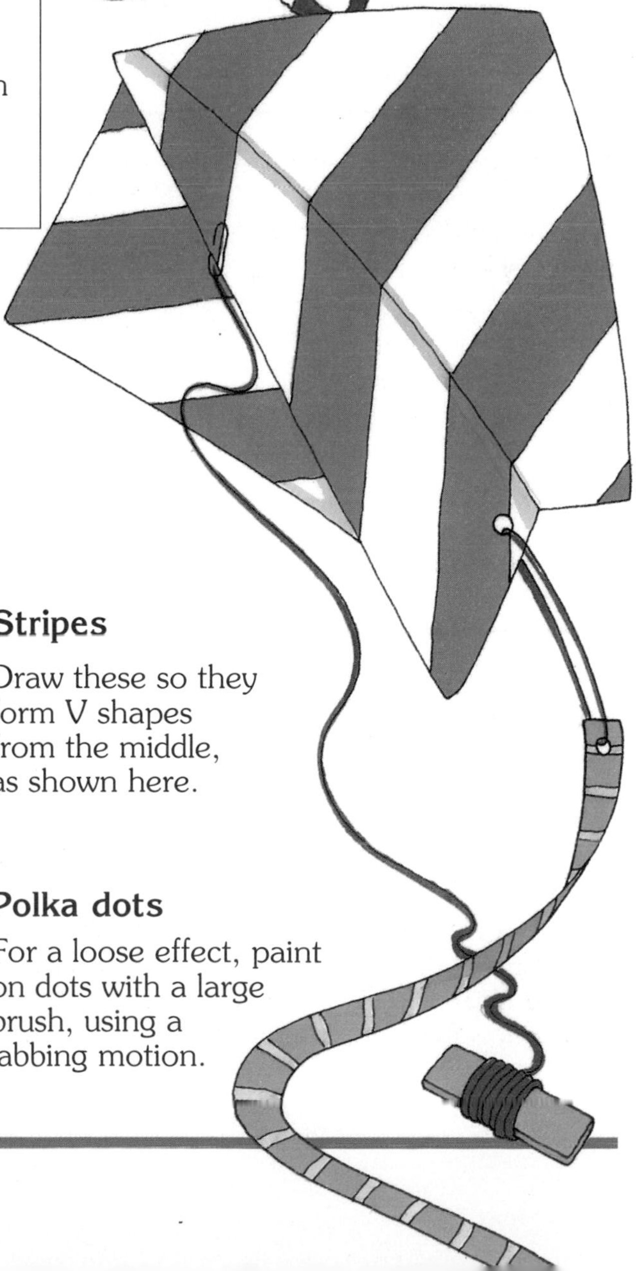

Flight tests

When your kite is finished, test fly it with the paper clip attached in different places. If the wind is gentle it will probably fly best if you position the paper clip on line A. Try it on line B if the breeze is a little stronger.

Decorative ideas

Dazzling stripes
You should use thick felt-tip pens to make this striking effect.

Stripes
Draw these so they form V shapes from the middle, as shown here.

Zebra stripes
Draw bold, sharp-edged, black swirling stripes on your kite.

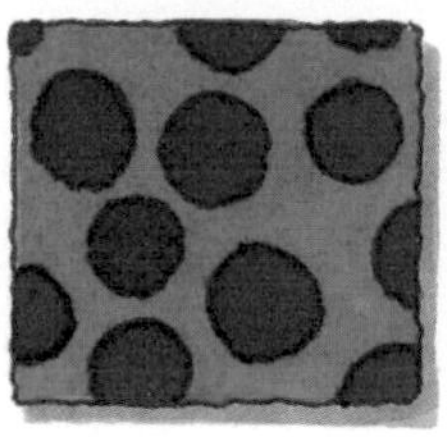

Polka dots
For a loose effect, paint on dots with a large brush, using a jabbing motion.

Tips and techniques

Tracing a template

 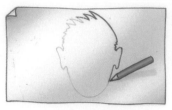  

1. Lay tracing paper over the template. Paper clip the tracing paper to the template. Trace the outline in pencil.

2. Unclip the tracing and turn it over. Draw over the outline in pencil, covering it thickly. Turn the tracing over again.

3. Lay the tracing on cardboard or paper. Go over the lines again, so that a line appears on the surface beneath.

4. Remove the tracing paper. You should see the tracing on the new surface. Go over the lines with a pencil or ball-point pen.

Papier mâché techniques

Making flour paste

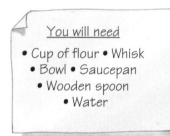

You will need
- Cup of flour • Whisk
- Bowl • Saucepan
- Wooden spoon
- Water

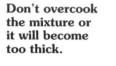

Don't overcook the mixture or it will become too thick.

This recipe will make enough paste for one papier mâché project. If you need more paste, increase the quantities accordingly.

1. In a bowl, whisk a cup of flour with a cup of water. Add two more cups of water and mix well to get rid of any lumps.

2. Put the mixture into a saucepan and bring it to the boil, stirring constantly. Then leave it to stand, so that it cools completely.

3. To store the paste, cover it tightly with some plastic food wrap and keep it in a refrigerator. It should last for several days.

Papier mâché pulp

This recipe will make enough pulp for one of the papier mâché plates on pages 34-35.

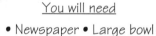

You will need

- Newspaper • Large bowl
- Large spoonful of PVA (household) glue mixed with a large spoonful of flour paste (see recipe above) • A strainer

1. Cut or tear several layers of newspaper into 1.5cm (½in) squares. Pack it tightly into a mug to fill it.

2. Soak the paper in hot water and leave it for three hours. Then knead it with your fingers to make a pulp.

3. Squeeze the water from the pulp through a strainer. Then put it in a bowl. Add a large spoon of glue and paste mix.

4. Knead it together well. Add more glue mix until it feels like soft clay. Store it in a bag in a refrigerator.

Scoring a line

When you need to make an accurate fold, score it first. Empty ball-point pens are the best for this. They run smoothly and do not scratch or rip the paper.

1. Put a ruler along the line you want to score. Hold it there firmly, to ensure that it doesn't slip when you draw your line on the paper.

2. Using a ball-point pen, draw a perfectly straight line against the ruler. Press hard to make a firm crease (exactly how hard you press depends on the paper's thickness).

Origami tips

Symbols

While you are doing the origami projects in this book you will see various symbols. These are used to signal various turns and folds that you need to do.

Turn the paper over.

Turn the paper around.

Fold then unfold the paper to make a crease.

Making a square of paper

You may need to start a project with a square of paper, although you don't have one. Here is an easy way that you can convert an oblong shaped piece into a square of paper.

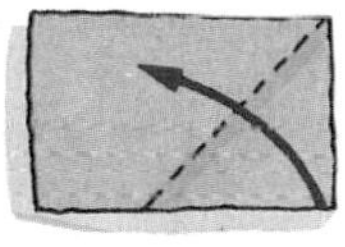

1. Fold the bottom corner up to the top edge to make a triangle.

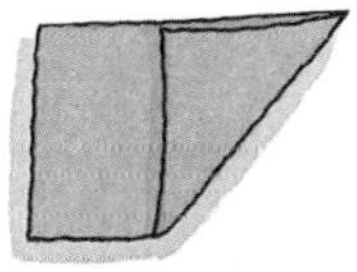

2. Cut along the side of the triangle that you have just made.

3. Open out the paper. You will have made a perfect square.

Finding a square's middle

1. Fold the paper in half from side to side. Then unfold it.

2. Fold the paper in half from top to bottom and unfold it.

3. The middle is where the creases meet.

The middle

Finding the middle of an edge

1. Fold the corners together and pinch in the middle.

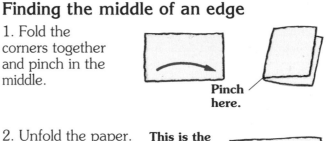

Pinch here.

2. Unfold the paper. The pinch mark will be in the middle of the paper.

This is the middle.

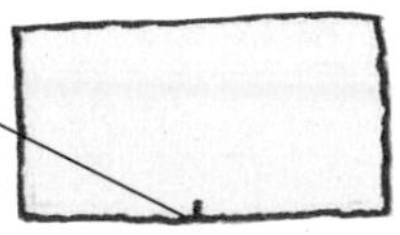

Folding tips

Follow these tips to help ensure that you always make neat, accurate folds.

• Always fold the paper away from you.

• Work on a hard surface, such as a table, and press firmly along each fold.

• Always make sure that corners and edges of your paper meet accurately before you press them down to make a fold.

• Follow all of the procedures that are shown in the picture on the right.

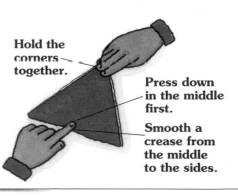

Hold the corners together.

Press down in the middle first.

Smooth a crease from the middle to the sides.

Balancing a mobile (page 22)

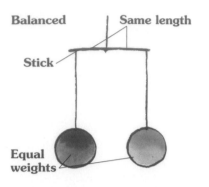

Balanced **Same length**

Stick

Equal weights

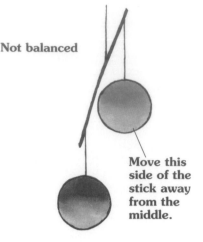

Balanced

Long arm   **Short arm**

Heavy weight

Light weight

Not balanced

Move this side of the stick away from the middle.

Parts of a mobile always work in this way: if both arms of a mobile (that is, the stick across the top that hangs out either side of the thread that it is suspended from) are the same length, they balance equal weights.

When parts of a mobile do not balance, move the middle thread very gradually to the end that is pointing down. Eventually, the weights will become balanced.

When you make a mobile you will need to balance each hanging piece one by one (once all the pieces are hanging from their threads). It won't take long.

Flying the kite (pages 84-85)

The best places to fly your paperfold kite are in open spaces such as fields. Check that kite flying is not forbidden in the place you want to visit. Take a friend to help you fly the kite. It's more fun to go with someone than going alone.

The best conditions are when there is constant, moderate wind and no rain. If the wind is strong it may rip your kite. If it rains the kite might be soaked, which could ruin the paper.

Launching the kite

1. Check that all the knots on your kite are secure before you launch it. If they are not tight the kite might break loose and blow away.

2. Stand with your back to the wind. Ask your helper to hold the kite up as shown in the right. Let out about 5m (16ft) of line.

3. Ask your helper to push the kite up into the air. As it rises, pull gently on the line. Try not to tug at the kite or the line might snap.

4. Slowly let out more line. If the kite starts to fall, pull the line gently. As it rises again, let out more line.

Flying alone

If you are flying the kite on your own, stand with the wind behind you. Hold the kite by its towing point, so it faces into the wind. Let out a little line with the other hand. Release the kite gently into the air. As the wind lifts the kite, steadily let out more of the line.

Bringing down the kite

Bring down the kite carefully. To do this, wind the line slowly around the reel, or ask your helper to pull the line down for you, while you wind it up in a ball. Make sure you don't tug the line too sharply or the line might snap.

Templates

The templates on the following eight pages are for you to trace and cut out, to make some of the projects shown in this book. Trace all the lines shown on the templates, then cut out the lines shown in red and score the ones shown in blue. If a template shows a green line, you should trace that line onto the fold of a folded piece of paper or cardboard.

Paper pencil tops (pages 10-11)

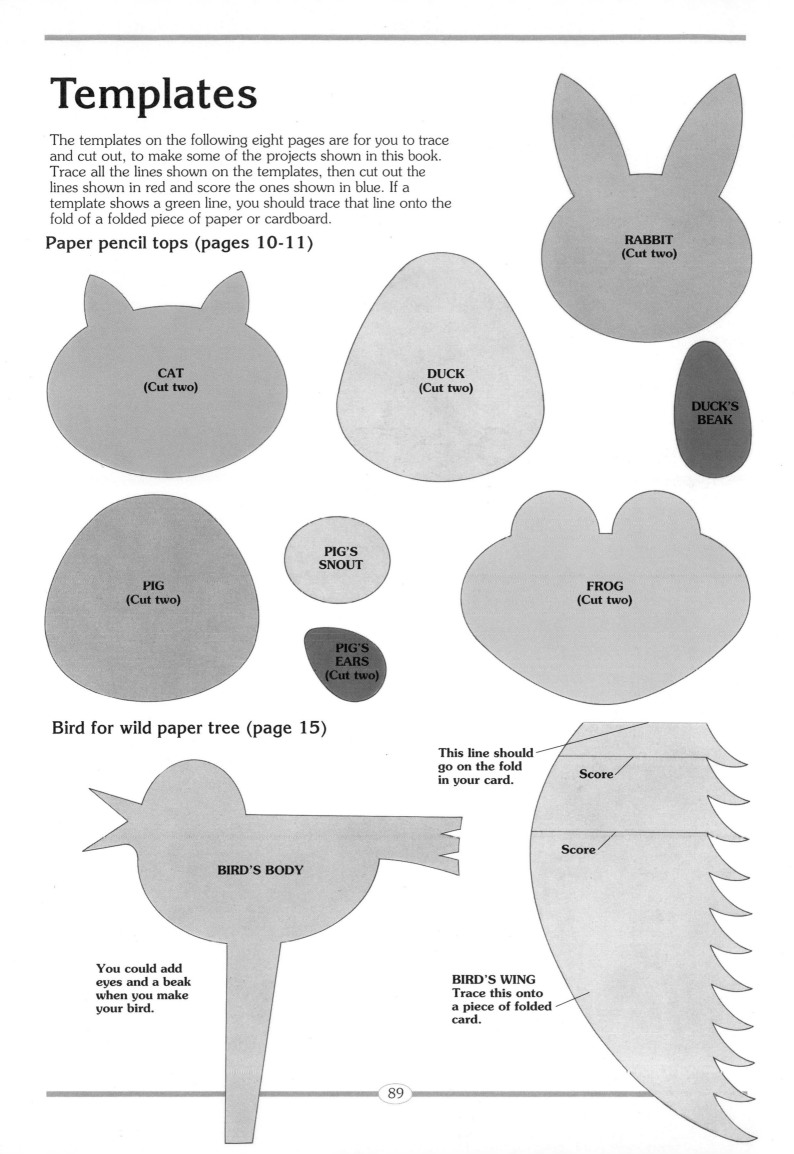

RABBIT
(Cut two)

CAT
(Cut two)

DUCK
(Cut two)

DUCK'S BEAK

PIG
(Cut two)

PIG'S SNOUT

FROG
(Cut two)

PIG'S EARS
(Cut two)

Bird for wild paper tree (page 15)

BIRD'S BODY

You could add eyes and a beak when you make your bird.

This line should go on the fold in your card.

Score

Score

BIRD'S WING
Trace this onto a piece of folded card.

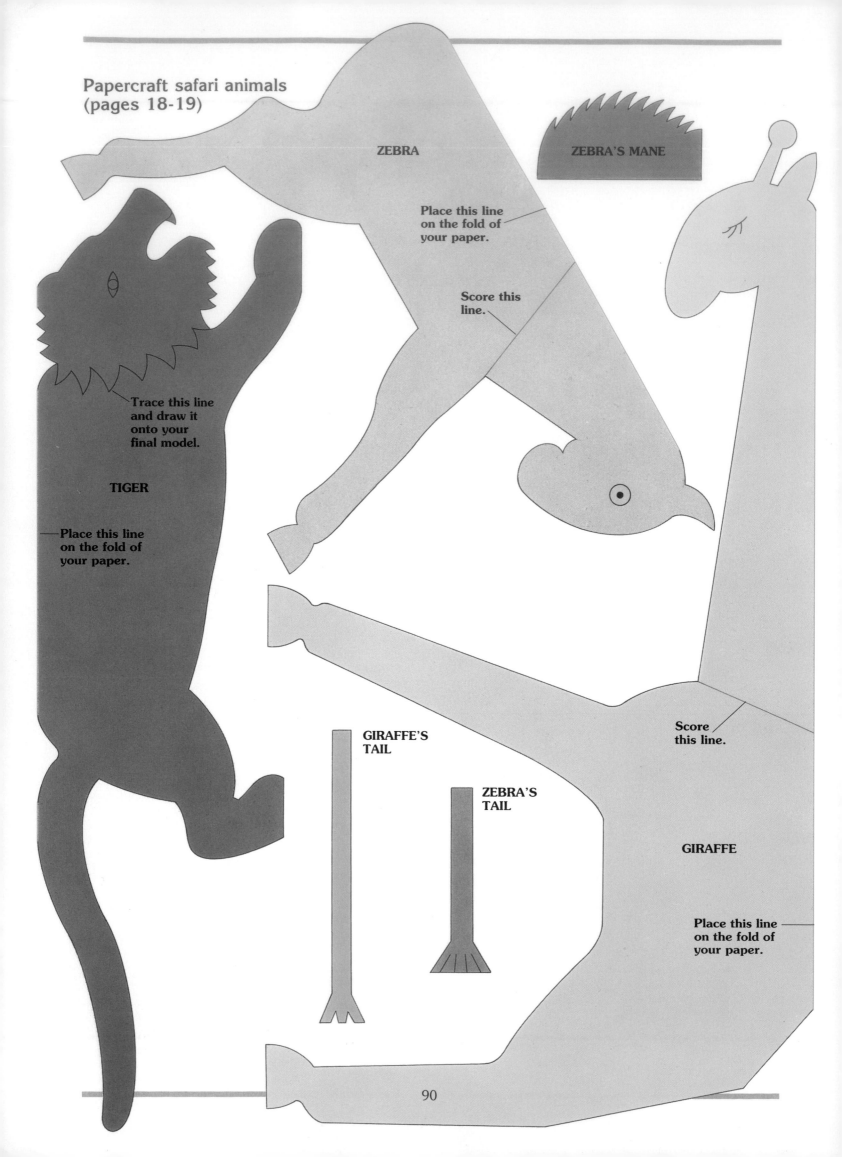

Papercraft safari animals
(pages 18-19)

ZEBRA

ZEBRA'S MANE

Place this line
on the fold of
your paper.

Score this
line.

Trace this line
and draw it
onto your
final model.

TIGER

Place this line
on the fold of
your paper.

Score
this line.

GIRAFFE'S
TAIL

ZEBRA'S
TAIL

GIRAFFE

Place this line
on the fold of
your paper.

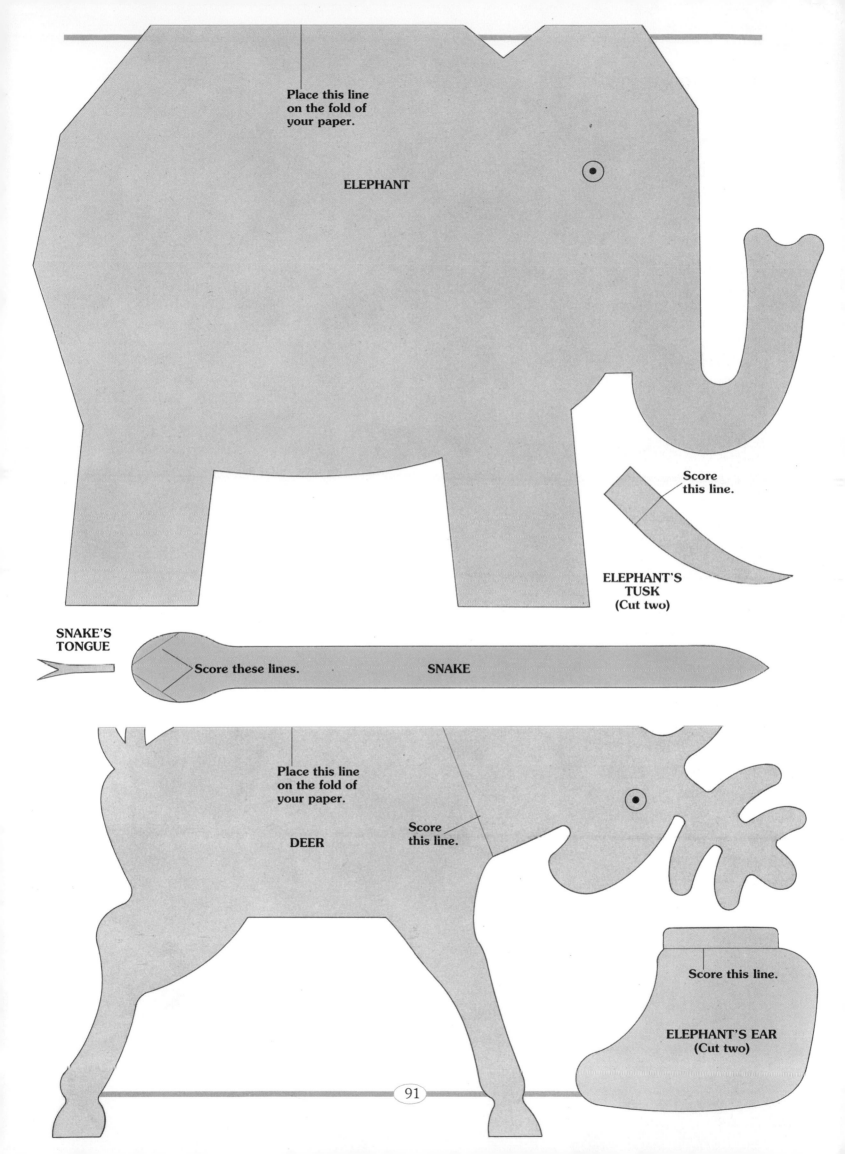

Place this line
on the fold of
your paper.

ELEPHANT

Score
this line.

ELEPHANT'S
TUSK
(Cut two)

SNAKE'S
TONGUE

Score these lines.   SNAKE

Place this line
on the fold of
your paper.

Score
this line.

DEER

Score this line.

ELEPHANT'S EAR
(Cut two)

Crocodile (pages 20-21)

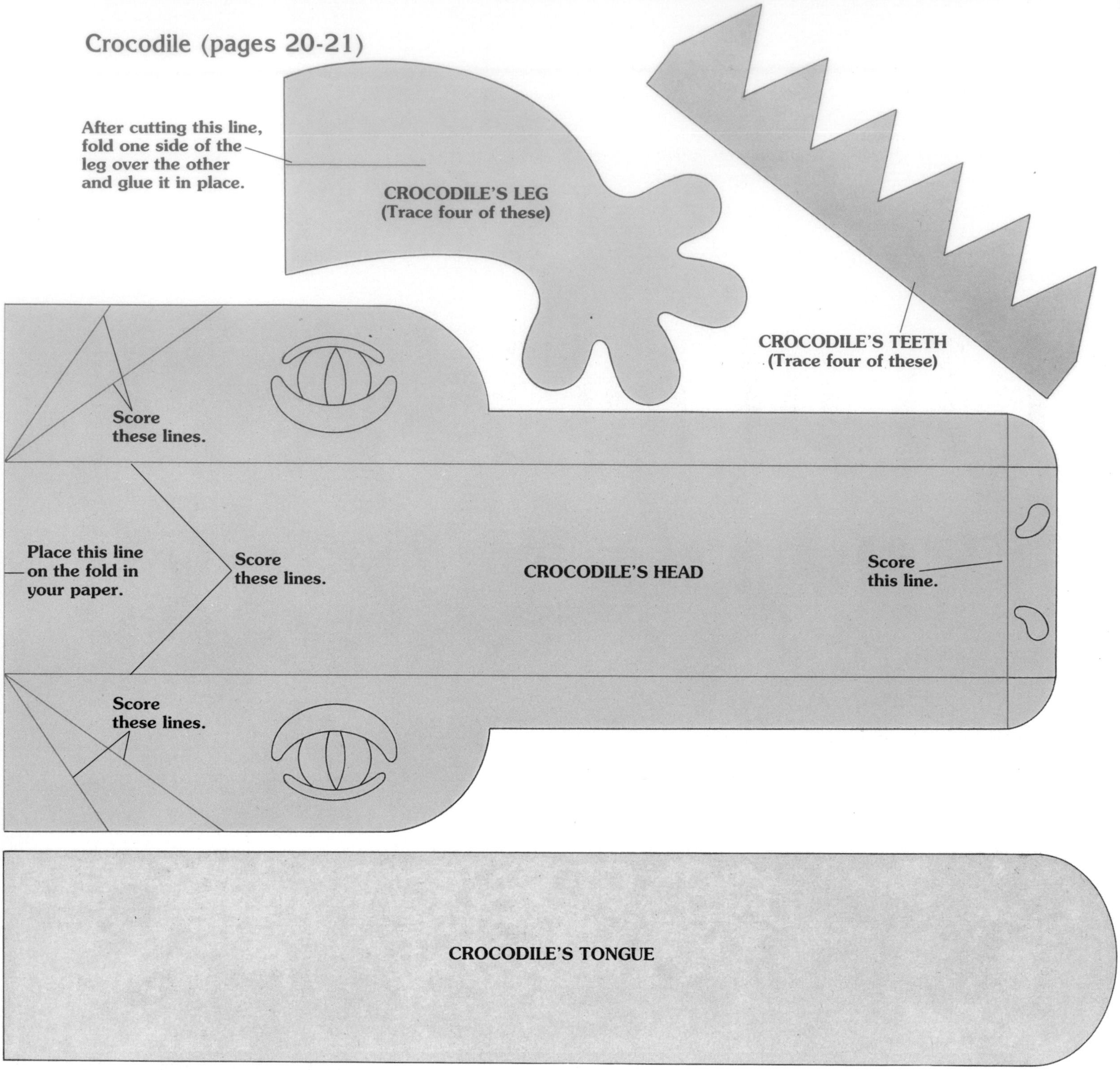

After cutting this line, fold one side of the leg over the other and glue it in place.

CROCODILE'S LEG
(Trace four of these)

CROCODILE'S TEETH
(Trace four of these)

Score these lines.

Place this line on the fold in your paper.

Score these lines.

CROCODILE'S HEAD

Score this line.

Score these lines.

CROCODILE'S TONGUE

Sunflower (pages 30-31)

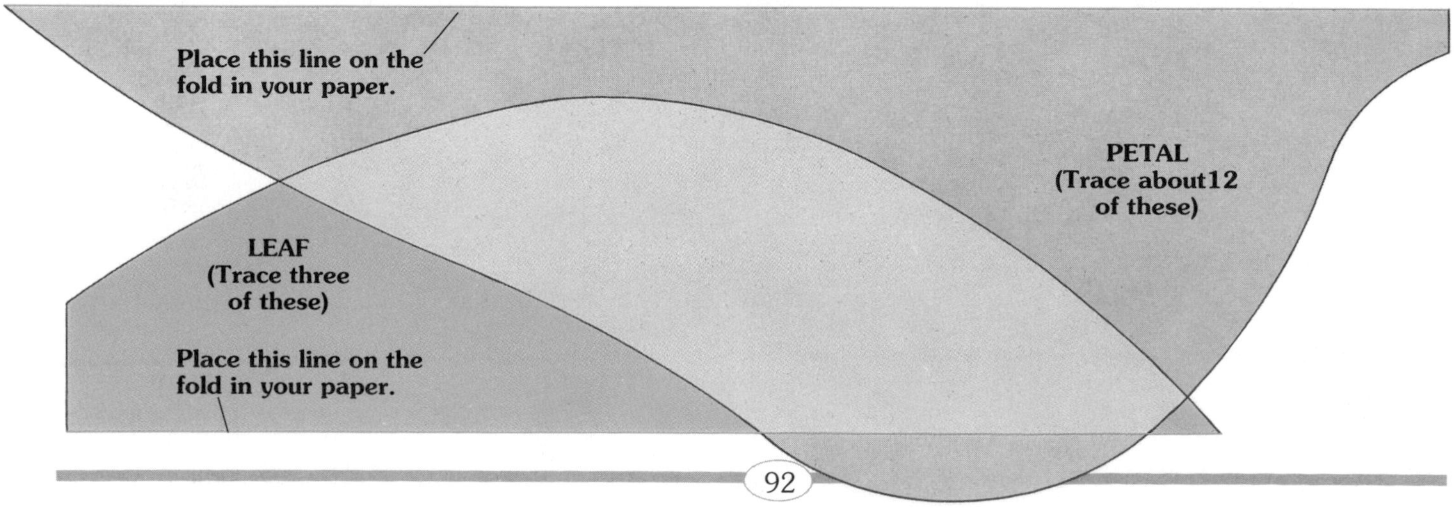

Place this line on the fold in your paper.

PETAL
(Trace about 12 of these)

LEAF
(Trace three of these)

Place this line on the fold in your paper.

Roman numerals (pages 36-37)

Trace these Roman numerals to put onto the clock face. You might also like to trace them to put on the gift boxes that you can make on pages 54-55.

If you want to trace the numerals smaller or larger than they are shown here, put this page on a photocopier (available for use at public libraries) and enlarge or reduce the page, then trace the resulting photocopy.

I II III IIII V VI VII

VIII IX X XI XII

Fancy lettering (from pages 54-55)

Trace these letters to put onto the gift boxes. If you want to trace them smaller or larger than they are shown here, put this page on a photocopier and enlarge or reduce the page, then trace the resulting photocopy.

A B C D E F G

h i j k l m n

o p q r s t u

v w x y z

Mask templates

Some of these templates show only half a mask. When you trace one of these, follow these instructions:

1. Fold tracing paper in half. Unfold it and place tracing paper on half-template, with fold on green line shown on template.

2. Trace over half-template, pressing down firmly all the time. Take tracing off half-template, fold tracing paper again, and turn it over.

3. Carefully trace outline onto other side of tracing paper.

Your template will now be complete and you can go on to make your mask.

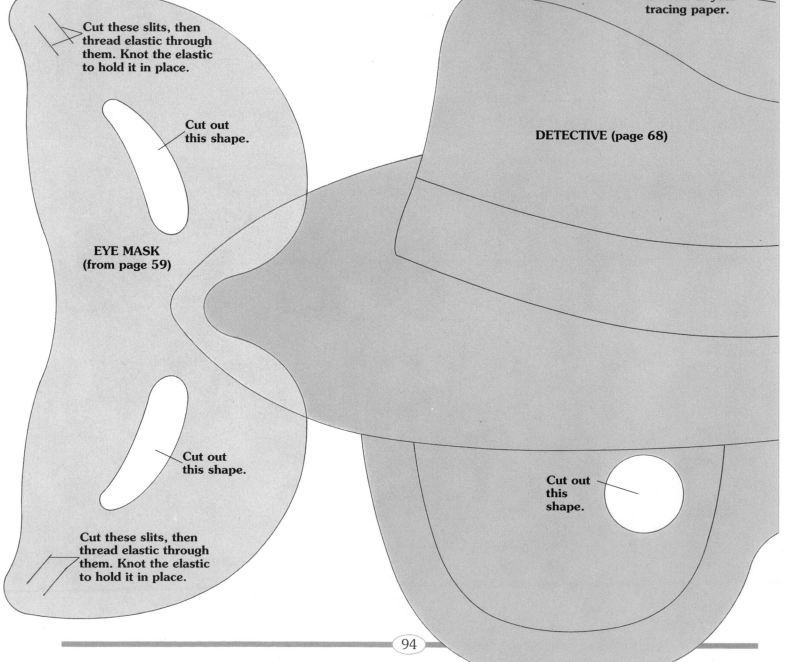

BEE MASK (page 62)
and
BASIC MASK
(pages 68 and 69)

Place this line on the fold in your tracing paper.

Cut these slits, then thread elastic through them. Knot the elastic to hold it in place.

Cut out this shape.

Score this line for the detective and movie star masks only.

Cut these slits, then thread elastic through them. Knot the elastic to hold it in place.

Cut out this shape.

EYE MASK (from page 59)

Cut out this shape.

Cut these slits, then thread elastic through them. Knot the elastic to hold it in place.

Place this line on the fold in your tracing paper.

DETECTIVE (page 68)

Cut out this shape.